HEALTH FINANCING AND DELIVERY IN VIETNAM

HEALTH, NUTRITION, AND POPULATION SERIES

HEALTH FINANCING AND DELIVERY IN VIETNAM

LOOKING FORWARD

by

SAMUEL S. LIEBERMAN

AND ADAM WAGSTAFF

THE WORLD BANK
Washington, DC

ISBN-13: 978-0-8213-7782-6
eISBN: 978-0-8213-7783-3
DOI: 10.1596/978-0-8213-7782-6

Library of Congress Cataloging-in-Publication Data

Lieberman, Samuel S.
Health financing and delivery in Vietnam : looking forward / by Samuel S. Lieberman and Adam Wagstaff.
    p. ; cm.
Includes bibliographical references and index.
 ISBN 978-0-8213-7782-6 (alk. paper)
1. Health insurance—Vietnam. 2. Medical care—Vietnam—Finance. 3. Health care reform—Vietnam. 4. Medical policy—Vietnam. I. Wagstaff, Adam. II. World Bank. III. Title.
 [DNLM: 1. Delivery of Health Care—Vietnam. 2. Health Care Costs—Vietnam. 3. Health Care Reform—Vietnam. 4. Health Expenditures—Vietnam. 5. Health Policy—Vietnam. 6. Insurance, Health—Vietnam. W 84 JV6 L716h 2009]
 RA412.5.V5L54 2009
 362.109597—dc22

                                                        2008041838

Contents

Tables

Foreword

Despite being a low-income country, Vietnam has gained significant improvements in the health field. The country's basic health indicators (infant, under-five, and maternal mortality) continue to fall and are comparable to those of countries with substantially higher per capita incomes. Vietnam has strongly emphasized the importance of equity in health with its series of pro-poor health policies, which should result in only minimal gaps in health outcomes between the poor and better-off. In some respects, it is believed that Vietnam has been quite successful in achieving this goal.

Furthermore, measures to strengthen the health system continue to be implemented. The social health insurance program now covers nearly half of the population, and the goal is universal coverage. Since 2002, the government has allocated a large budget each year to the so-called Health Care Fund for the Poor, which buys health insurance cards for the poor and selected ethnic minorities. The near-poor are also to be subsidized to the tune of 50 percent of the voluntary health insurance premium.

In addition to direct support on the demand side, the government has also implemented measures to strengthen the supply side of the health system, for example, upgrading commune health centers and district and provincial hospitals; supporting the development of preventive health centers; implementing policies to attract health workers to rural areas and train health workers serving disadvantaged communities; and granting health facilities greater autonomy.

Vietnam still faces challenges in health care. While there is clarity on the goals of the government's policy on health—equity, efficiency, and development—there is an ongoing debate about how best to achieve some of these goals. This reflects the complexity and the difficulty of the challenges ahead, but also the government's need to feel its way on the issue of the appropriate role of market mechanisms in a pro-poor health sector.

This World Bank study therefore comes at an opportune moment. It focuses on the challenges facing our health financing and health service delivery systems. It provides not only new analytic work, but also new ideas about how to address some of the key issues that the health sector is facing. We welcome the study and look forward to a continued fruitful engagement with the World Bank on Vietnam's health system development in the coming years.

Dr. Nguyen Hoang Long
Deputy Director, Department of Planning and Finance
Ministry of Health, Vietnam
August 2008

Acknowledgments

The study benefited from many forms of collaboration with the Vietnamese government; we are particularly grateful for the guidance provided by Drs. Lieu and Long (Director and Deputy Director, respectively, of the Department of Planning and Finance, Ministry of Health). We are also grateful for helpful comments, advice, and support throughout the course of the study from: Lisa Studdert of ADB; Susan Elliott of AusAid; and Dr. Graham Harrison, Henrik Axelson, and Nguyen Kim Phuong of WHO. Staff at the World Bank's Hanoi office—notably Carry Turk, Huong Lan Dao, Mai Thi Nguyen, Nga Nguyet Nguyen, Nga Quynh Nguyen, and Thu Thi Minh Nguyen— provided extensive help and support for which we are grateful. Joseph Capuno provided extensive contributions to the study, which substantially improved its quality. Jack Langenbrunner, Panagiota Panopoulou, and Pia Schneider kindly served as peer reviewers, and Toomas Palu generously provided comments on an earlier draft. The study was undertaken under the general supervision of Ajay Chhibber (former County Director, Vietnam), Emmanuel Jimenez (Director, East Asia & Pacific Region Human Development Sector), Fadia Saadah (former Sector Manager, East Asia & Pacific Region Health, Nutrition & Population), and Martin Rama (Vietnam, Lead Economist).

Samuel S. Lieberman
Adam Wagstaff
September 2008

Overview

Background

Vietnam's successes in the health sector are legendary. Its rates of infant and under-five mortality are comparable to those of countries with substantially higher per capita incomes, and it has brought down child mortality far faster than might be expected for a country with its per capita income. Maternal mortality has also fallen dramatically, as have deaths from communicable diseases. It is true that Vietnam has done less well than some neighboring countries in certain areas—tuberculosis, for example, has fallen faster in many neighboring countries—and there are concerns over new and re-emerging communicable diseases such as HIV/AIDS, Avian flu, Japanese encephalitis, and severe acute respiratory syndrome (SARS). It is also true that, like other growing economies, Vietnam has seen a growth of noncommunicable diseases such as cancer, cardiovascular disease, and diabetes. But as this book shows, Vietnam's legendary performance continues. Vietnam saw reductions in age-specific mortality rates between 2000 and 2005 for all ages, while some of its neighbors saw little change or even increased rates for some ages. By 2005, Vietnam's age-specific death rates compared favorably with those of Malaysia—a far richer country—across all ages. And for people below the age of 55, Vietnam's age-specific mortality rates were far better than those of Thailand.

Why then the need for a further study on Vietnam's health system? The answer is that while Vietnam has done and continues to do better than might be expected, given its per capita income, its health system could probably do better. Vietnam is not alone in this regard. Indeed, the health systems of *all* countries could probably do better. Vietnam is only now about to make the jump from a low-income country to a middle-income country. But the challenges that its health system has faced for several years are largely the challenges of a middle-income country. For example, by international standards, Vietnam has a high incidence of catastrophic household health spending—a large fraction of households make out-of-pocket payments for health care that exceed a reasonable fraction of their income. This reflects two facts: People in Vietnam are receiving quite sophisticated care, but the country's social health insurance program does not yet cover the entire population. Achieving universal coverage, which is the government's goal, and reforming other elements of the health care financing and delivery systems so that people receive timely care in a non-hospital setting where possible, and providers are incentivized to treat patients in a cost-effective fashion, are middle- and upper-income country challenges. Yet Vietnam is making fast progress rising to these challenges right now, even though it has not quite passed the per capita income threshold that would put it in the club of middle-income countries.

This book reviews Vietnam's successes and the challenges it faces, and goes on to suggest some options for further reforming the country's health system. Options for expanding coverage to 100 percent of the population are compared. The issue of how to deepen coverage—so that insurance reduces out-of-pocket spending by more than it does at present—is also discussed, as is the issue of how to put downward pressure on the cost of health care. The book also looks at the issues of how to improve the quality of care, both overall and at the hospital level, and how to reform provider payment methods. It also looks at the issue of stewardship—what different *parts* of government (the Health Ministry, the health insurer, and so on) should be doing at each level of government, and what different *levels* of government (the central government, provincial government, and so forth) ought to be doing.

Evolution of Vietnam's Health System

Vietnam's health sector has witnessed some dramatic changes during the last 50 years. From independence in 1954 to unification in 1975, the country successfully pioneered free publicly provided primary health care and categorical programs. However, unification in 1975 posed major challenges for the health sector—emigration of skilled medical staff from the south, a slowdown in the economy, resources being spread more thinly to build up the network of facilities in the south, among other things—and the sector started deteriorating. In the late 1980s the government launched its *Doi Moi* reforms, which were highly successful at rejuvenating the economy. They also had a direct and an indirect effect on the health sector by stimulating reforms within the sector. Income growth had a favorable impact on child malnutrition and mortality, and the additional resources in the health sector increased contact and bed occupancy rates, which had previously fallen. Out-of-pocket spending on health care increased dramatically, reaching 71 percent of total health spending in 1993; most of the spending was on drugs rather than fees.

The 1990s saw a variety of additional measures, some aimed at containing the growth of out-of-pocket spending. The central government assumed responsibility for paying the salaries of commune health center (CHC) workers, who had previously relied upon sales of drugs and medicines for their income; the effect was to reduce the share of revenues in CHCs coming from drug sales. Fee waivers were introduced, though they appear to have been only weakly targeted on the poor and were largely ineffective, mainly because people were largely spending their money on drugs rather than fees. The government also introduced a schedule of fees and charges for tests, and a health insurance program, aimed initially at formal sector workers. The government also increased its supply-side subsidies to the health sector. However, despite these measures, out-of-pocket spending as a share of total health spending continued to rise, reaching 80 percent in 1998. In contrast to the early 1990s, fees made up a sizable share of spending, yet still accounted for a minority of expenditures.

In the early to mid-2000s, further reforms occurred. The central government launched its Health Care Fund for the poor program, which provides insurance coverage for the poor and other disadvantaged groups, including ethnic minorities living in disadvantaged provinces. The central government provided resources to provinces to enroll the target groups in the health insurance scheme, but gave provinces the option of delivering free care to the target groups and reimbursing providers for the lost income. The central government indicated its preference for the insurance modality, but half of provinces opted to reimburse providers directly. During this period, several other important changes occurred in health insurance: copayments were scrapped and the benefit package made more generous in other ways; all formal sector workers were required to enroll, rather than just those in large institutions; and the insurer was permitted to contract with private providers. The health sector was decentralized during this period. Much of the revenue was already being raised locally, and the reform ensured that the level of government where revenues were being raised was also the level where decisions were being taken. Subsequent reforms aimed at reducing the reliance of local governments on their own resources through more generous and more redistributive transfers, some earmarked for specific programs, including the aforementioned Health Care Fund for the Poor program. Also during the 2000s, the health sector gradually implemented two decrees aimed at giving public sector service providers greater autonomy, including over their financial affairs. Finally, the government launched a major program, with donor support, to upgrade CHCs, intercommune polyclinics, and district hospitals.

Yet more changes are planned. The price schedule is to be uprated, that is, brought in line with today's prices, some hospitals are to be given even greater autonomy, and the government is making adjustments to its insurance program and completing an insurance law, which includes the aim of expanding coverage. One quandary facing government is that the revision of the price schedule and the granting of even greater autonomy to providers will surely put upward pressure on out-of-pocket spending, while the government's efforts in relation to insurance may or may not succeed in expanding and deepening coverage.

Health Financing and Delivery in Vietnam Today

Vietnam spends around 5 percent of its GDP on health, with 75 percent of revenues being raised through out-of-pocket payments (figure 1). Over half of these are payments to public providers, one-quarter are for drugs, and the remainder (17 percent) are to private providers, mostly private clinics (figure 2). While total health spending in Vietnam is broadly in line with expectations, based on the cross-country relationship between GDP per capita and health spending, Vietnam's government health spending is considerably less than "expected." This reflects a relatively small share of government expenditure being allocated to the health sector, rather than a small share of GDP being absorbed by government spending. The latter is considered to be broadly sustainable from a fiscal perspective. Most government spending is allocated at the provincial level or below, but roughly one-third of a province's spending comes from central government transfers. These are increasingly redistributive, and are sizable.

Figure 1: Revenue Sources in Vietnam's Health System, 1998, 2000, and 2005

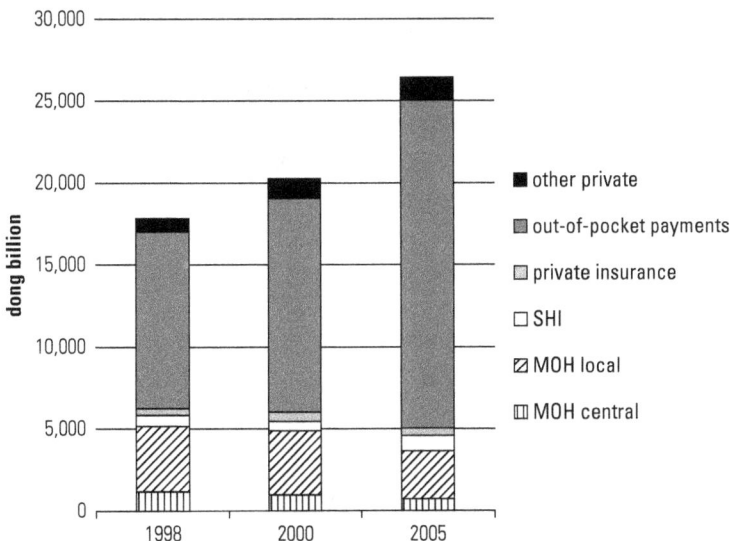

Source: Vietnam National Health Accounts, available from World Health Organization NHA Web site, and Knowles et al.

Figure 2: Out-of-Pocket Health Spending, Vietnam 2006

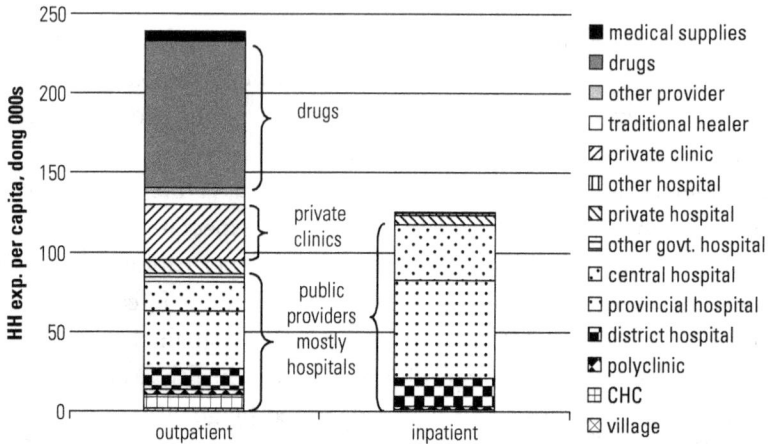

Source: VHLSS 2006.

Most general government health spending is still on supply-side subsidies, with the social health insurance (SHI) program accounting for just 10 percent of total health spending. The supply-side subsidies are absorbed mostly by urban hospitals, while SHI enrollments and outlays are highest among the better-off, reflecting higher enrollments among the better-off formal sector workers. Unsurprisingly, Vietnam scores fairly badly by regional standards in terms of the degree to which government health spending reaches the poor (figure 3). SHI enrollment is not only higher among the better-off, but at 40 percent it still covers less than one-half of the population, well below the 100 percent target of the government. That said, the recent expansion of coverage among the poor has helped to both raise enrollment and narrow the gap between poor and rich (it is the middle-income groups that have the lowest enrollment rates now).

Vietnam's provider payment methods are a mix of budget (still dominated by bed norms) and fee-for-service, with prices fixed by the government in 1995. There has been very little experimentation with prospective payments. In terms of provider organization, the public sector still operates the pyramid structure developed after independence—CHCs, intercommune polyclinics, district hospitals, provincial hospitals, and national hospitals. CHCs are widespread

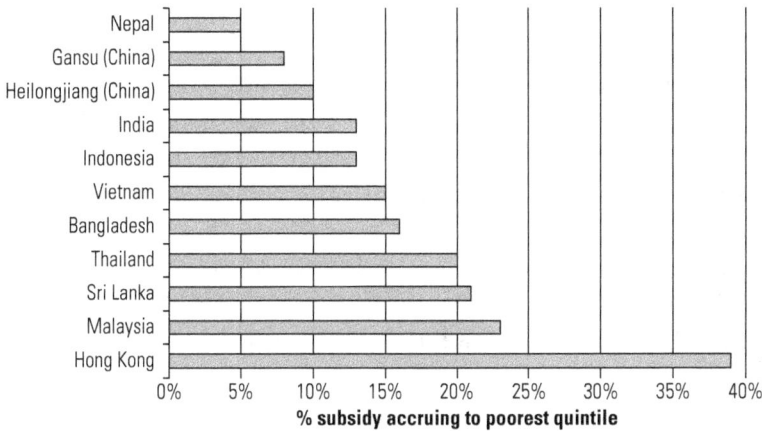

Figure 3: Who Benefits from Government Health Spending in Vietnam?

% subsidy accruing to poorest quintile

Source: O'Donnell et al.

(on average each serves just 7,000 people), but users are disproportionately poor and the facilities are underused. Hospitals, in contrast,
are heavily used, with bed occupancy rates (calculated on allowable
beds) often exceeding 100 percent. These utilization patterns reflect
the perception that the quality of care is lower in CHCs, and the fact
that the price differential allowed under the official price schedule is
relatively small. The public sector has been the subject of an extensive modernization program, and public providers have been granted
increased autonomy under the autonomization program. The private
sector appears to have grown in recent years, with drug vendors and
general practitioner clinics being the largest groups of registered private providers. Research suggests that many private providers are not
registered with the government as they are required to be, however,
and that at least in one province there may be twice as many private
providers as public providers.

Trends in Vietnam's Health Sector Performance

Ultimately, the goal of any health sector is to improve population
health. The study finds that on child mortality, Vietnam has done
well, even when its performance is adjusted for its recent rapid

growth. Its achievement with regard to age-specific mortality for all causes of death also looks rather good (figure 4). Unlike Thailand, which saw rising age-specific mortality rates at some ages between 2000 and 2005, and Malaysia, where the decline in age-specific mortality appears to have stagnated, Vietnam saw reductions between 2000 and 2005 in age-specific mortality at all ages. Furthermore, by 2005, Vietnam's age-specific death rates compared favorably with those of Malaysia across the full range of ages. But on other health indicators Vietnam has done less well: the incidence of fever and acute respiratory infections among children increased between 1998 and 2002, while in Indonesia and the Philippines it fell; and Vietnam has lagged behind Cambodia, China, Indonesia, and the Philippines in reducing tuberculosis prevalence and mortality.

It is not just average health outcomes that matter, but inequalities, too. The study finds that inequalities between the poor and better-off in infant and under-five mortality have continued to widen in Vietnam, while in the Philippines and Indonesia they have either narrowed or increased only marginally. Geographic inequalities are evident, too, and are widening: Vietnam's richer south and Red River Delta have reduced infant mortality faster than the poorer central and northern regions of the country.

Figure 4: Trends in Age-Adjusted Mortality—Vietnam Compared to Malaysia and Thailand

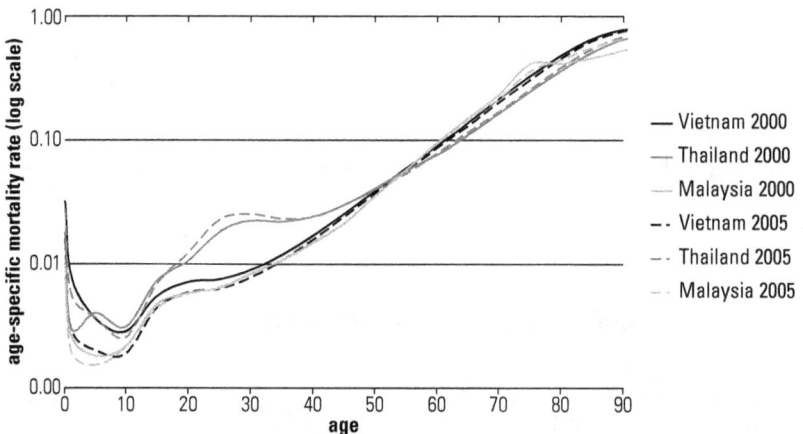

Source: WHO Life Tables for Member States http://www.who.int/whosis/database/life_tables/life_tables.cfm.

Health systems are, of course, not just about improving health. Good ones also organize the financing of health services in such a way that people are protected from the financial consequences of illness and death. The study finds that Vietnam fares rather badly by international standards in terms of the proportion of the population experiencing catastrophic health expenses—expenses exceeding a certain percentage of nonfood consumption (figure 5). It also finds that while Vietnam's performance on this yardstick improved during the 1990s, it has not apparently done so during the 2000s. The study also finds that inpatient expenses account for only half of the spending of households experiencing catastrophic spending, with the other half due to the steady drip-drip-drip of spending on drugs and outpatient visits. Recent increases in the incidence of catastrophic spending have been most pronounced in the southeast and Mekong Delta.

Figure 5: Catastrophic Household Health Expenses, Vietnam and Other East Asian Countries

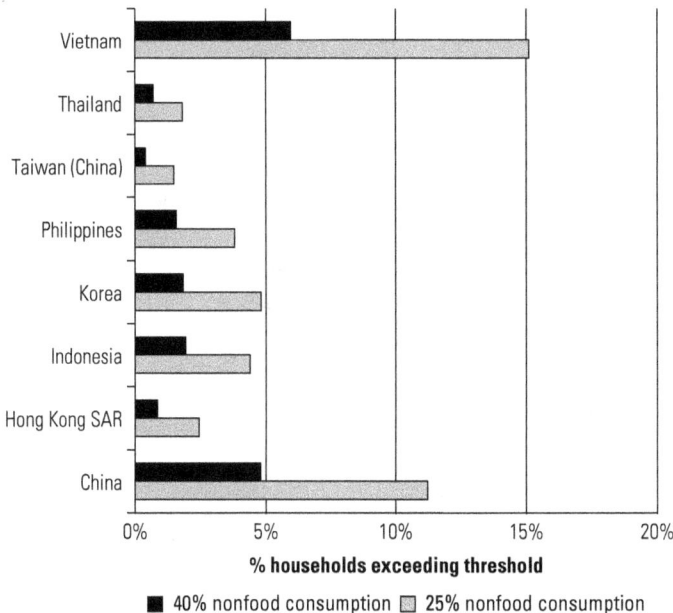

Source: Van Doorslaer, O'Donnell, et al.

Health Insurance

Health insurance has been identified by policy makers as very important in Vietnam—rightly so, given the potential impact of insurance on the use of services and financial protection. The study finds that insurance coverage has increased considerably over the last few years, and has risen rapidly recently with the launch of a tax-financed program for the poor (figure 6). There are, however, substantial numbers of people among each target group who have no coverage—not even a health card (figure 7). The groups that are relatively easy to identify for tax-financed support (the poor, people living in officially designated disadvantaged communes, ethnic minorities living in mountainous regions) are already largely covered, while those who are relatively easy to coerce into contributing (workers in the formal sector) are mostly contributing. Noncoverage is most pronounced among harder-to-identify and harder-to-coerce groups. The pace of

Figure 6: Trends in Insurance Coverage through VSS, Vietnam 1993–2006

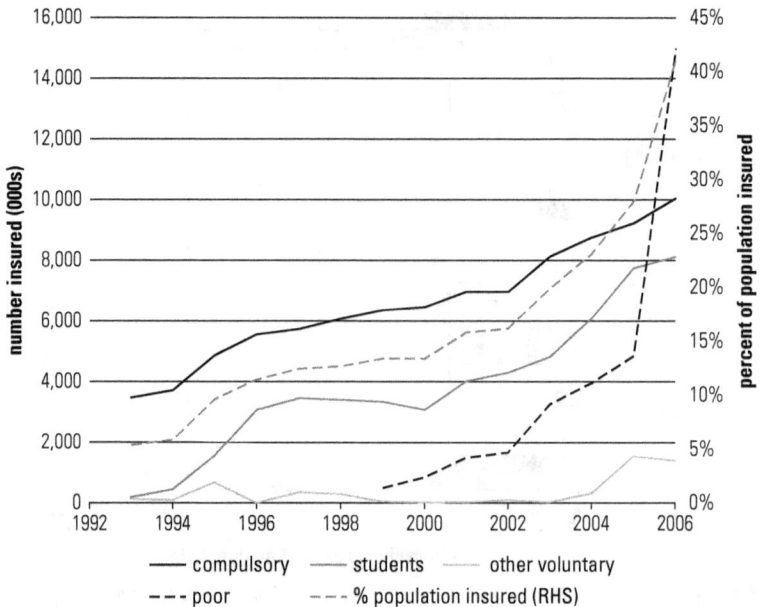

Source: Vietnam Social Security (VSS).

Figure 7: Enrollment Numbers by Target Group, 2006

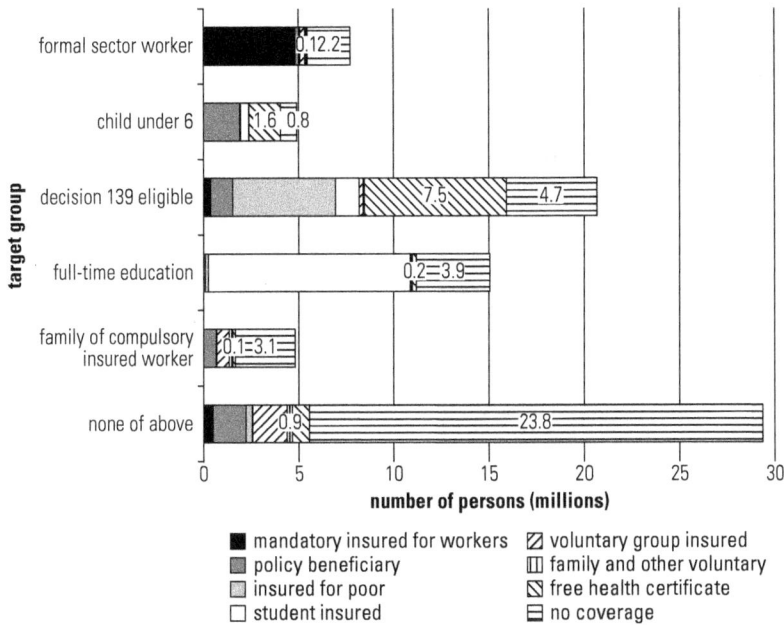

Source: Authors' calculations from 2006 Vietnam Household and Living Standards Survey.

expansion seen in recent years will not continue, and coverage expansion is likely to return to its former slow pace.

Insurance has increased utilization of services, but has had only a modest effect on out-of-pocket spending, that is, it has provided only limited financial protection. This reflects in part the fact that the insurer, Vietnam Social Security (VSS), reimburses only a part of the provider's costs (40 percent of the population is covered by insurance, but insurance accounts for only 13 percent of total health spending), with the rest covered by supply-side subsidies and out-of-pocket payments. As regards the financial sustainability of the insurance program, the last few years have seen the scheme's surplus turn into a deficit, with no signs of a turnaround. Both adverse selection and moral hazard appear to be contributory factors in cost escalation, and tackling both is a major policy challenge on top of the challenges of expanding and deepening coverage.

Reforming Health Insurance

Vietnam's health insurance system faces three major challenges: expanding coverage to a larger section of the population; deepening coverage so that patients pay a smaller fraction of the cost out of pocket; and containing costs. There is no agreement internationally on how best to do these things. The book explores three options: expanding coverage within the existing policy framework; moving toward a mandatory contributions-based scheme for everyone except the poor, who would continue to be financed at taxpayers' expense, as at present; and a universal program with formal sector workers contributing according to their earnings and everyone else's coverage financed at taxpayers' expense.

The fiscal implications of the third option are explored in some depth. They turn out not be as daunting as one might expect, due in part to Vietnam's small fiscal deficit, and in part to the fact that the government is credibly committed to expanding its revenues through a broadening of its revenue base. General government spending on health (inclusive of VSS contributions) would rise by a total of D 76,000 per capita, or D 6.3 trillion in aggregate (table 1), pushing general government expenditure on health as a share of GDP from 1.5 percent to 2.2 percent—still below its "expected" share on the basis of international experience. If this extra spending were financed entirely through additional borrowing, Vietnam's fiscal deficit would increase from 3.8 percent of GDP to 4.4 percent of GDP. But because households would spend less out of pocket on health care, there is a case for raising taxes as a quid pro quo. The expanded personal income tax, which comes into force in 2009 and which is projected to raise an extra D 14 trillion, is one option. A full-fledged property tax is another. In contrast, increasing cigarette taxes would raise relatively little revenue (Van Kinh et al. 2006), because of the high price elasticity of demand for cigarettes in Vietnam, with people switching in response to price increases to other (largely untaxed) forms of tobacco, including chewing tobacco (Ramanan Laxminarayan 2004).

The book also looks at options for deepening insurance coverage. This requires that someone other than the patient pick up a larger

Table 1: Simulating the Costs of Universal Insurance

Population 82.48 million

GDP per capita dong 11,806,000

	CURRENT (2006)	100% COVERAGE, ADDITIONAL COVERAGE FINANCED BY GOVT. SPENDING, CURRENT DEPTH OF COVERAGE	100% COVERAGE, ADDITIONAL COVERAGE FINANCED BY GOVT. SPENDING, DOUBLE VSS REVENUES
VND billions			
Government expenditures on budget support (supply-side)	9,000	9,000	9,000
Government expenditures on subs to HI (demand-side)	3,155	9,973	19,946
Voluntary contributions	520	0	0
Earnings-related contributions	2,129	2,129	4,259
Out-of-pocket payments	29,901	26,664	14,561
Total	*44,706*	*47,766*	*47,766*
OOP share (%)	67%	56%	30%
VSS outlays	5,804	12,102	24,205
Government expenditures on health care	12,155	18,973	28,946
General government expenditures on health care	14,804	21,102	33,205
Overall government expenditures including VSS contributions	267,600	273,898	286,000
Extra general government expenditures compared to current		6,298	18,400
VND 000's per capita			
Government expenditures on budget support (supply-side)	109	109	109
Government expenditures on subs to HI (demand-side)	38	121	242
Voluntary contributions	6	0	0
Earnings-related contributions	26	26	52
Out-of-pocket payments	363	323	177
Total	*542*	*579*	*579*
VSS outlays	70	147	293
Government expenditures on health care	147	230	351
General government expenditures on health care	179	256	403
Overall government expenditures including VSS contributions	3,244	3,321	3,468
As % GDP			
General government expenditures on health care	1.5%	2.2%	3.4%
Private expenditures on health care	3.1%	2.7%	1.5%
Overall government expenditures including VSS contributions	27.5%	28.1%	29.4%
Fiscal deficit (current, and for scenario if extra spending financed through borrowing)	−3.9	−4.4	−5.7
Government revenues (current, and for scenario if extra spending financed through higher revenues)	27.1	27.8	29.0

fraction of the provider's costs. It could be achieved by increasing supply-side subsidies. Or it could involve an upward revision of the fee schedule that governs the prices that insured and uninsured patients pay providers. If a large fraction of the population is left uninsured, raising fees is an unattractive option; more generous supply-side subsidies would help reduce out-of-pocket payments for both insured and uninsured patients. The problem with this approach is that it reduces the scope for VSS to leverage cost reductions and quality improvements. If, in contrast, most if not all of the population is covered, increasing fees is an attractive option because it means that more of a provider's income comes from VSS, and VSS has increased leverage over providers. As VSS pays more of the cost, the need for facilities to charge patients out-of-pocket payments is reduced.

Raising VSS contributions in the hope of deepening coverage would have public expenditure implications, of course. For example, in the third option above, if as well as expanding coverage to the currently uninsured at the taxpayers' expense, the government were also to double VSS revenues (a doubling of contributions from formal sector workers and a doubling of demand-side subsidies to cover others), government spending would increase by D 18.4 trillion rather than by D 6.3 trillion (the rise if coverage were expanded but not deepened; see table 1). General government spending on health would reach 3.4 percent of GDP, a little above the "expected" fraction. If financed through higher government revenues, the share of GDP absorbed by taxes, fees, and grants would increase to 29 percent (currently it is 27 percent). The doubling of VSS revenues would leave out-of-pocket payments accounting for 30 percent of total health spending, or more if providers were successful at holding on to their out-of-pocket payment income *and* getting the higher fee income from VSS.

The book also looks at cost-containment strategies for the insurance program. On this issue, there is no consensus internationally. There is disagreement, for example, on the effectiveness of copayments as a tool for tackling moral hazard, and on what ought to be included in a benefit package. In contrast, there is considerable agreement that certain ways of paying providers do better than others at promoting cost-consciousness. There is also an emerging consensus that clinical guidelines may play an important role in containing costs. These strategies all have implications for the way health care providers operate, and are therefore *both* health financing *and* service delivery issues.

Service Delivery

The *Doi Moi* reforms of the 1980s started a process of considerable change among Vietnam's health providers. Budget support was cut, and facilities were allowed to charge patients directly, retain user fee revenues, and, subject to limits, use these revenues to pay staff (mostly through higher bonuses, but also through the hiring of contract staff). Amid concerns of health care becoming unaffordable, Vietnam in the mid-1990s put in place a set of fees and charges, which is in practice a mixture of per-diem rates and fees per item of service. This schedule has remained largely intact ever since, although procedures that did not exist at the time have been priced at prevailing values rather than 1995 values, and the prices of drugs are not regulated at all. Only very limited attempts have been made to depart from this payment model. The most recent reform initiative took the form of Decree 10—revised and given even more "teeth" in Decree 43—which required that service delivery units (SDUs) across the whole of government become more financially self-sufficient. SDUs have been encouraged to earn more income from clients and to use these extra revenues to pay higher salaries to staff, with the presumption being among commentators that budget support will be scaled back even further in due course.

In terms of performance, the study finds that the quality of care for mothers and small children seems to have improved, and is good by international standards. However, the study also finds that costs in the hospital sector are rising rapidly, and the bulk of the annual increases *cannot* be explained by increases in throughput. There are growing concerns about the quality of care and whether all care delivered is actually medically necessary. It is also clear that, despite the growth of outpatient visits recently (figure 8), the delivery system is overly biased toward inpatient care, reflecting Vietnam's poorly developed primary care system.

Figure 8: Trends in Inpatient Admissions and Outpatient Visits

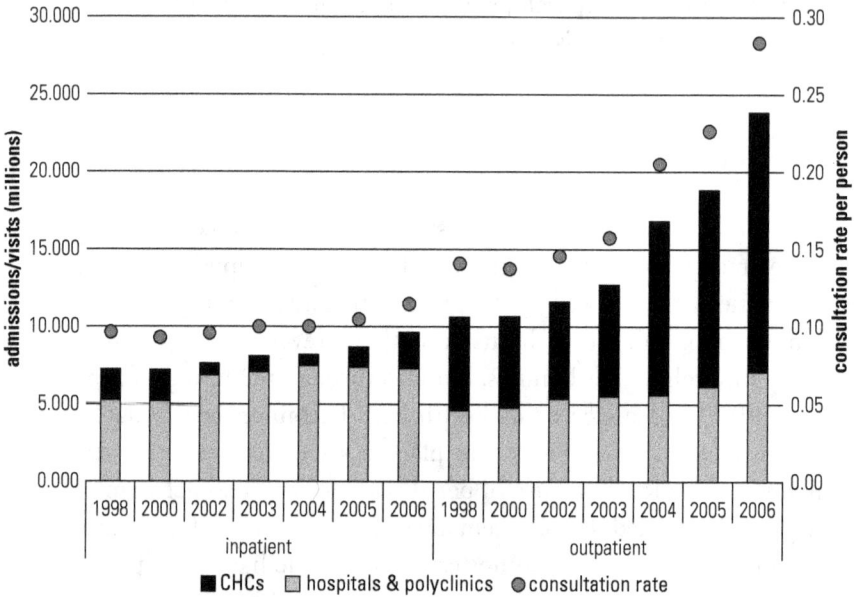

Source: MOH Health Statistics Yearbook various years.

The rapid growth of costs owes much to the perverse incentives caused by the mixture of budgets and fee-for-service (FFS), the latter being the payment method for both VSS and the uninsured. Figure 9 shows how the revenue mix of hospitals divides across budget revenues, fee income from patients, and revenues from VSS. Budgets, being based on bed norms, encourage hospitals to jealously guard their bed stock and put patients in beds even if they could be treated at a lower-level facility or on an outpatient basis. FFS encourages providers to deliver more services, whether or not the services are medically necessary. The health insurance agency (VSS) plays a very limited role as an informed "purchaser" of health services: It acts largely as a passive payer of bills, and in any case picks up only 13 percent of total health expenditures. Supply-side subsidies in the form of state budgets are also paid in a passive way, in line with bed norms. Neither VSS nor the states exercise much financial control over providers. Nor do they have measures in place to assure the quality of care. Patients are thus left largely to fend for themselves. But patients are poor "consumers" when it comes to health care because

Figure 9: Source of Hospital Revenues, Vietnam 1998–2005

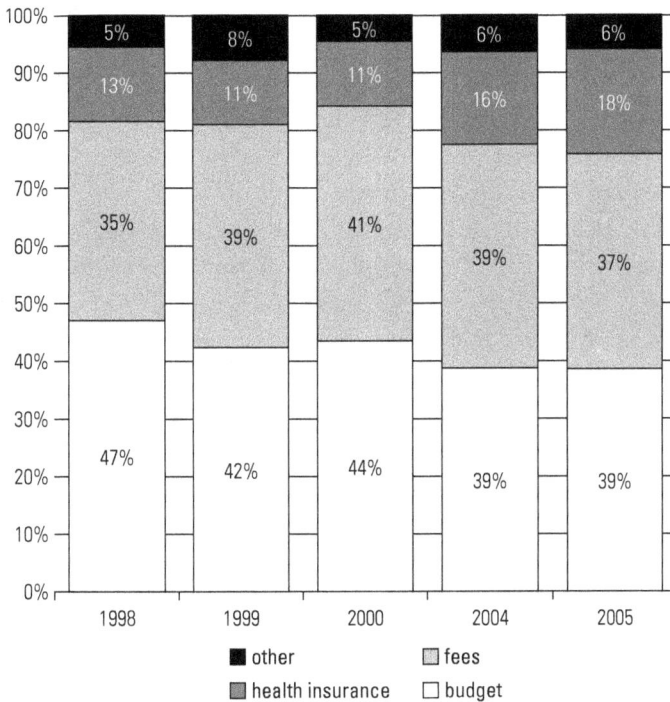

Legend:
- ■ other
- ☑ health insurance
- ☐ fees
- ☐ budget

Source: Calculations from Vietnam hospital inventory.

of their limited knowledge of medical matters. The scope for providers to induce demand for unnecessary care is high when they are paid on a FFS basis and are given strong incentives to generate revenues. Yet this is precisely the direction in which Decrees 10 and 43 have pushed the sector. The book presents evidence that is consistent with the idea that Decrees 10 and 43 have indeed encouraged hospitals to earn more user fee income, but they have also raised costs, especially administrative costs. Nothing, regrettably, can be said using existing data about their impacts on the quality of care.

Reforming Service Delivery

The book argues that clinical guidelines have the potential to improve quality and reduce costs by curbing unnecessary care. But for this to happen there must be incentives for providers to follow the guidelines. If following guidelines means losing revenue, providers are unlikely to follow them. "Carrots" and "sticks" can both be used. The obvious "stick" is to reduce payments to providers that do not adhere to the guidelines. This is more easily done if there is one payer, VSS. If VSS can detect noncompliance with the guidelines, it could reduce the payment to the provider for the case. In the scenario where VSS, the Ministry of Health (MOH), and patients all pay some money to the provider, the issue arises of who will identify noncompliance. Patients, as the biggest payer, have the strongest incentive, but they are in the weakest position to do so.

The book argues that "clinical pathways" are a promising way of operationalizing clinical guidelines, and allow VSS and the patient to easily detect providers' noncompliance with clinical guidelines. Pathways are a simple document—a single form—that shows the steps to be taken in treating a patient with a given diagnosis and how soon after admission the steps should be taken. When there is a single payer (for example, VSS in the universal coverage scenario), the pathways form provides a highly valuable tool for auditing. Bills could be linked to the diagnosis, and the care that has been delivered can be checked against the care package identified for a standard case in the pathway form. Clinical pathways are being developed specifically for Vietnam by MOH through a bottom-up consultative process with select hospitals. To date, only a few diagnoses are being worked on, and progress is methodical but slow. It might make sense to begin with pathways developed in other countries, and have committees of experts (including representatives from senior hospital management) adapt them to the Vietnamese setting. It is also important that VSS be involved in the process so that it can start to develop a pathway-based auditing system.

The book also looks at the options for reforming the way providers are paid. The most obvious reforms are to shift to a case-based payment system (such as diagnosis-related groups or DRGs) for hospitals, and a mix of capitation and FFS (for preventive interventions) for lower-level providers. These changes could, in principle, be implemented in the current multiple-payer system where out-of-pocket payments dominate. However, they are far more likely to be successful in a single-payer system, where VSS covers the entire population and pays for the bulk of health care costs. Vietnam appears, in fact, to be committed to case-based payments, and is exploring the feasibility of basing the rates on a cost analysis of the care associated with the clinical pathway for each case type. Compared to a statistical analysis of existing costs by case type, this has the merit of providing a "gold standard," indicating the costs associated with care delivered according to best practice clinical decision making. Given the slow progress on developing clinical pathways, however, it might make sense to take a DRG system that has been developed for another country (most have their origins in the United States' DRG system) (Schreyogg et al. 2006) and modify it to the Vietnamese setting. Over time, as the clinical pathways work proceeds in Vietnam and elsewhere, the DRG rates could be modified accordingly. One challenge here will be Vietnam's hospital information system, which lacks discharge-level data, including ICD-9-CM diagnosis and ICD procedure codes that are essential for DRG use. Vietnam may also want to explore rewarding hospitals with additional payments if they score well on a battery of quality indicators. This system, known as pay for performance, or P4P, is a supplementary payment method, not a replacement for case-based payments.

Finally, on the issue of provider reform, the report looks at the issue of provider autonomy. The appropriate direction of reform depends crucially on the degree to which Vietnam is successful in its goal of universal coverage under a single payer. With a single payer that picks up the bulk of health care costs, patients have a strong champion of their interests. If the payer has a quality control mechanism in place and a payment system that incentivizes cost containment and high-quality care (for example, a mix of case-based payment and P4P), it makes good sense for health facilities to have a fairly strong financial incentive to treat more patients and improve quality. The payer would award contracts to facilities that meet the payer's cost and quality standards, and the contracts would reward volume (extra cases not extra services) and high quality. In such a system, the scope for providers to earn additional income by delivering care that is medically unnecessary is limited. It is right and proper in such a system that providers should be incentivized to earn additional revenues, which they can do by treating extra patients and improving quality. Providers should also be encouraged in this scenario to have a good deal of latitude over personnel and investment decisions. If they employ cheap but underqualified staff, they will risk forgoing quality-related payments. If they invest in expensive but unnecessary diagnostic equipment, they will incur additional costs that will not be covered by the case-based payment. With a strong "purchaser" and the right incentives, providers ought to be granted autonomy in most areas. It is no accident that countries shifting away from a budget-based payment system have also taken steps to autonomize health providers. In this scenario, Decrees 10 and 43 are very much along the right lines.

In contrast, in a system such as the present one in Vietnam, where the patient is the main payer, provider autonomy can spell disaster for the patient and the health system. Providers who are underqualified and deliver poor-quality care are less likely to be brought to account in such a system. Providers who invest in expensive equipment and deliver unnecessary diagnostic tests may fool patients into believing that they are providing high-quality care, while in reality they are merely increasing their incomes at the patient's expense. China's health system during the 1990s and early 2000s provides a salutary reminder of what can happen when providers (even if nominally public) are given strong incentives to generate revenues in an environment where the patient is the main payer and oversight by the government is limited.

Decentralization and Government Stewardship

The study argues that the role of government in Vietnam's health sector is likely to change over the next few years. The Ministry of Health and the health departments of provincial governments still see themselves essentially as the financiers and operators of the supply side of the health system, although much of the supply side is not public, much of the public sector enjoys considerable autonomy, and providers are increasingly drawing their revenues from insurance reimbursements and out-of-pocket spending, rather than supply-side subsidies. The central government has also been slow to respond to the decentralization of power to the provinces: The Health Ministry acts as if the health sector were simply *administratively* deconcentrated and required to follow central directives.

At each level of government, the responsibility of government is likely to change over the next few years. VSS will increasingly be seen as a "purchaser" and less as a passive payer of bills. This will require a major change of approach by VSS, and an upgrading of capacity and information systems. At the same time, there will be less emphasis within the Health Ministry structure on financing and managing health facilities, and increased emphasis on stewardship activities: policy making; quality control in both the public and private sectors, including licensing, accrediting, and the development of clinical guidelines; helping to set up new provider payment mechanisms; the provision of information to the population and to other actors in the health system; monitoring and evaluation; and so on. Other actors will also play a role in the stewardship of the sector: the health insurer has a role to play in promoting quality care that is affordable; professional organizations have a role to play in developing and enforcing good practices; boards of directors have a potential role to play in the oversight of providers, as well as the insurer; and consumer watchdog groups have a role to play in helping to promote cost-consciousness and good practices.

The responsibilities of different levels of government are likely to change, too. The gradual shift from supply-side financing to demand-side financing will strengthen the role of the insurer as a financing agency and reduce that of the Health Ministry, and especially that of the health department at the provincial level. Given the centralization of the health insurance program, decision making will inevitably shift to the center, at least with regard to health insurance. This will accentuate the current tendency for the poor to subsidize the rich within the program. This tendency could be reduced by having providers paid on a standard per-case basis rather than according to the services actually delivered. But there is also scope for allowing some local decision making in the size of the benefit package by allowing provinces to top up the nationwide minimum coverage through locally raised resources, at least up to a ceiling. There is also scope within the remaining supply-side subsidies (for example, for public health) for the central government to condition its allocations to local governments on the achievement of certain targets, rather than simply handing over the money, as at present.

Looking Ahead

There are some issues that the book discusses, but not in great depth. The most obvious is the role of the private sector—including drug vendors. This has received comparatively little attention in Vietnam from either researchers or policy makers. Yet it is clear that the people of Vietnam make heavy use of the private sector and that it absorbs a large fraction of out-of-pocket spending on health. The private sector's size is also most likely underestimated by official statistics due to underregistration by private providers. Work geared toward better understanding the private sector and thinking through its future relationship with the public insurance system and the public delivery system is likely to have a high payoff.

Further work is also clearly needed on developing *the specifics* of the ideas developed in the report: how to implement the various ideas for expanding and deepening coverage; how to design and implement prospective payments; how to transform VSS from a passive payer of bills into a strategic purchaser; how to think through exactly what different parts and levels of government ought to be charged with in the health sector; and how to design and implement the appropriate accountability relationships. These issues are all interrelated and need to be tackled in tandem. As was once said in a report by The Reforming States Group in 1998: "The health care system is like a fabric woven from many different threads. One cannot work on the fabric one strand at a time; instead, one must work on the whole cloth." There is a need to think simultaneously about expanding coverage (via one of the three options set out in the book), deepening coverage (the best bets, arguably, being to uprate the fee schedule, raise VSS revenues, and get providers to lower their charges to patients), and implementing measures on both the demand and supply sides that will exert downward pressure on costs and upward pressure on quality (provider payment reform that encourages cost-effective care by all providers, the development of skilled and incentivized providers out-side hospitals, and the use of quality assurance methods, including by the main payer, VSS). The tools elaborated in the book are already under development in Vietnam, but progress to date has been slow, in part due to the lack of capacity and inadequate data. Rectifying these shortcomings is essential, but it is more likely to happen if there is greater clarity of the roles and responsibilities in the health sector of different parts of government at each level of government and of different levels of government (for example, central vs. provincial). Health reform is not a purely technical exercise; it is as much about capacity, responsibilities, and accountability.

CHAPTER 1

Vietnam's Health System Since *DOI MOI*

Vietnam's successes in the health sector are legendary and were rightly emphasized in *Growing Healthy* (World Bank 2001), the 2001 report produced jointly by the World Bank, Sida, AusAid, and the Dutch Embassy. Vietnam's rates of infant and under-five mortality are comparable to those of countries with substantially higher per capita incomes, and it has brought down child mortality far faster than a country with its per capita income might have been expected to do. Maternal mortality has also fallen dramatically, as have deaths from communicable diseases. It is true that Vietnam has done less well than some neighboring countries in some areas—tuberculosis, for example, has fallen faster in many neighboring countries—and there are concerns over new and re-emerging communicable diseases such as HIV/AIDS, Avian flu, Japanese encephalitis, and SARS. It is also true that, like other growing economies, Vietnam has seen a growth of noncommunicable diseases such as cancer, cardiovascular disease, and diabetes. But as this report shows, Vietnam's legendary performance continues. Vietnam saw reductions in age-specific mortality rates between 2000 and 2005 for all ages, while some of its neighbors saw increased rates for some ages, or little change. By 2005, Vietnam's age-specific death rates compared favorably with those of Malaysia—a far richer country—across all ages. And for people below the age of 55, Vietnam's age-specific mortality rates were a good deal better than those of Thailand.

Why then the need for a further World Bank study on Vietnam's health system? The answer is that while Vietnam has done and continues to do better than might be expected, given its per capita income, its health system could probably do better. Vietnam is not alone in this regard. Indeed, the health systems of *all* countries could probably do better. Vietnam is only now about to make the jump from a low-income country to a middle-income country. But the challenges that its health system has faced for several years are largely the challenges of a middle-income country. For example, by international standards, Vietnam has a high incidence of catastrophic household health spending—a large fraction of households make out-of-pocket payments for health care that exceeds a reasonable fraction of their income. This reflects two facts: people in Vietnam are receiving quite sophisticated care, but the country's social health insurance program does not yet cover the entire population. Achieving universal coverage—the government's goal—and reforming other elements of the health care financing and delivery systems so that people receive timely care in a nonhospital setting where possible, and providers are incentivized to treat patients in a cost-effective fashion, are middle- and upper-income country challenges. Yet Vietnam is making fast progress with them right now, even though it has not quite passed the per-capita income threshold that will put it in the club of middle-income countries.

This book reviews Vietnam's successes and the challenges it faces, and goes on to suggest some options for further reforming the country's health system. Options for expanding coverage to 100 percent of the population are compared. The issue of how to deepen coverage, so that insurance reduces out-of-pocket spending by more than it does at present, is also discussed, as is the issue of how to put downward pressure on the cost of health care. The report also looks at the issues of how to improve the quality of care, overall and at the hospital level, and how to reform provider payment methods. It also looks at the issue of stewardship—which part of government at each level of government should be doing what in relation to the health system, and what different levels of government ought to be doing. These issues are all interrelated and need to be tackled in tandem. As the authors of a *Health Affairs* article on the United States once remarked (The Reforming States Group 1998): "The health care system is like a fabric woven from many different threads. One cannot work on the fabric one strand at a time; instead, one must work on the whole cloth." The issues also are ones where there is ample experience from middle- and upper-income countries on which to draw. But as these experiences show, including those of the Organisation for Economic Co-operation and Development (OECD) countries (Docteur and Oxley 2003), although there are some common trends in health system reform, there are many unresolved issues, and political economy and implementation challenges abound.

The Evolution of Vietnam's Health System

During the last 50 years or so, Vietnam's health sector has witnessed some dramatic changes (Vietnam MOH/Health Partnership Group 2008). From independence in 1954 to unification in 1975, the country successfully pioneered free publicly provided primary health care and categorical programs; these measures—along with the high level of literacy, especially among women—are considered responsible for Vietnam's spectacular reduction in child and maternal mortality during this period (World Bank 1992).

Unification in 1975 posed major challenges for the health sector: large numbers of physicians and other skilled health workers who had worked in private practice in the south left the country; resources in the north were stretched as efforts were made to build up a network of grassroots facilities in the south at a time when multilateral aid dried up and aid from the Eastern Bloc was being directed to sectors other than health; finally, high inflation (reaching 400 percent per annum at its peak) and a slowdown in economic growth (8.4 percent in 1984, but just 3.3 percent in 1986) reduced the resources going into Vietnam's health sector (World Bank 1992; Witter 1996; Sepehri et al. 2003). The mid- to late 1980s saw year-on-year real reductions in government spending on health, and it is likely that health infrastructure and health care began to deteriorate during the 1980s as a result of resources being cut back and spread more thinly (World Bank 1992). Inpatient admissions per capita, for example, started declining in 1980 and continued to decline each year until 1992, while consultations per capita began declining in 1984 (World Bank 2001).

During the late 1980s, the government launched its *Doi Moi* liberalizing economic reforms aimed at rejuvenating the economy. They included the decollectivization of agriculture, tax reform to expand revenues, reduced government spending, the closure and selling off of unprofitable state-owned enterprises and the downsizing of remaining ones, currency reform and international trade liberalization, and an encouragement of the private sector (Glewwe 2003). The effects of these reforms on economic growth and poverty appear to have been considerable: GDP growth jumped from 4.2 percent in the mid-1980s to 6.9 percent from 1988 to 1994, and to 7.4 percent from 1994 to 2000; meanwhile, the rate of poverty fell from 75 percent in 1984 to 58 percent in 1993, and then to 37 percent in 1998 (Glewwe 2003).

As part of these general reforms, the government also introduced liberalizing reforms in the health sector, broadly along the lines advocated by health sector staff of the World Bank at the time (De Ferranti 1985). Chief among them were the introduction of user fees and the sale of drugs in public facilities, and the legalization in 1989 of private medicine (including drug stores).

These reforms—and the *Doi Moi* reforms more generally—had several consequences for health sector outcomes. The improvements in living standards had beneficial knock-on effects for health outcomes: stunting among under-five children fell from 50 percent in 1993 to 35 percent in 1998 (Glewwe 2003); child mortality continued to fall after the introduction of the *Doi Moi* reforms and may have fallen faster after their introduction (Wagstaff and Nguyen 2003). The hospital bed occupancy rate started increasing immediately (from 1991 onward), and consultations per capita also began to increase, albeit not until 1993 (World Bank 2001). Public sector contacts per capita grew between 1993 and 1998, by 13 percent per year on average in the case of public hospitals and 10 percent annually in the case of CHCs (World Bank 2001). Contact rates in the private sector grew even faster, by 20 percent per annum in the case of private clinics, 25 percent per annum in the case of drug vendors, and 53 percent per annum in the case of traditional healers (World Bank

2001). Reassuringly, growth rates were similar across all income groups (World Bank 2001).

A further consequence of *Doi Moi* in the health sector was the rapid growth of household out-of-pocket spending. This was part of the so-called socialization of health care. As in China, the decollectivization of agriculture removed the main financing pillar of the primary health care system, namely revenues from the local agricultural commune. Commune health center (CHC) employees, as a result, looked to drug sales and fees to keep CHC revenues (and their incomes) constant. Drug sales in general, fees in public facilities, and private medicine all contributed to a rapid growth of out-of-pocket spending on health. By 1993, out-of-pocket spending accounted for 71 percent of total health spending, a major break with the past (World Bank 2001).

It was not long before Vietnam's central government introduced a variety of policy adjustments.

• Beginning in 1991, it introduced national target programs (NTPs) aimed at specific public health problems. Targets were set and resources were allocated strategically across different parts of the country. NTPs have survived—albeit with variations over time— to the present day, and have become a policy instrument by which the central government has attempted to exert influence over local governments in spending and priority setting.

• In 1994, the central government also assumed the responsibility for paying the salaries of CHC employees who had previously been paid by their commune (the responsibility passed to the provincial government in 2002). Government spending on CHCs more than doubled between 1994 and 1995, and the markup on drugs fell (in one study the share of CHC worker income financed through drug sales fell from 13.5 percent in 1991 to 6.4 percent in 1995) (Government of Vietnam-Donor Working Group on Public Expenditure Review 2000; World Bank 2001; Glewwe 2003).

• In 1995, the central government introduced a schedule of user fees for consultations and physical examinations, inpatient days, technical services, and lab tests; drugs are not covered by the schedule. While some variations were permitted by type of facility and area of the country, the aim was to ensure a broadly common set of user fees, rather than allowing facilities to charge whatever the local market would bear.

- In the early 1990s, local governments also began to introduce fee waivers for certain groups. However, these appear to have been usually only weakly targeted to the poor, and relatively ineffective at reducing out-of-pocket spending, not least of all because most of the out-of-pocket spending at the time was on drugs, not fees (World Bank 2001).

- In 1993, the central government launched a national health insurance program, initially covering civil servants, formal sector workers, and "people of merit" on a mandatory basis, and hoping to cover others on a voluntary basis (World Bank 2001). The program was slow to take off, however, and in 1997 coverage stood at just 12 percent of the population (World Bank 2001).

- Finally, the government increased its budget support to health facilities: supply-side subsidies increased by an average rate of 12 percent per annum in real terms during the 1990s, with central government outlays increasing fastest (14 percent per annum). The government also looked to the international community for financial assistance: development assistance to the health sector grew by an average rate of 10 percent per annum in real terms over the same period (World Bank 2001).

Despite these measures, however, out-of-pocket spending as a share of health spending continued to grow, reaching 80 percent by 1998 (Government of Vietnam-Donor Working Group on Public Expenditure Review 2000; World Bank 2001). The bulk of this spending was still on drugs, but between 1993 and 1998, fees increased as a share of out-of-pocket spending: rising in public hospitals from 6 percent to 53 percent, in CHCs from none to 26 percent, and in private clinics from 4 percent to 39 percent.

Changes in Vietnam's health sector continued through the mid- to late 1990s and early 2000s.

- Government responsibilities in health and other sectors were increasingly decentralized, with the 1996 and 2002 state budget laws giving local governments increased rights and responsibilities in the planning and execution of spending decisions (Lieberman et al. 2005). These measures essentially aligned spending and revenue-raising responsibilities more closely: resources for health were already largely locally generated (provincial spending has accounted consistently for around three-quarters of government health spending since the early 1990s), but local governments were restricted—at least notionally—by old spending norms from the years before *Doi Moi* (Lieberman et al. 2005). The new rules gave local governments more freedom in setting priorities in health, and between health and other sectors, and in the way provinces allocated resources across districts and communes.

- Accompanying these changes, however, was the introduction in 2004 of a formula-based intergovernmental equalization mechanism aimed at redistributing national resources for recurrent and capital expenditures more equally and more transparently across provinces and in support of national policy objectives (World Bank 2007).

- Another major initiative of the early 2000s in Vietnam in general was the push toward the autonomization of public service providers. The Health Ministry was initially somewhat lukewarm about the idea, fearful about the consequences of a shift of influence over the delivery system from the ministry to the free market. Autonomization was therefore introduced gradually from 2002 onward. Autonomized hospitals have been given greater control over their spending, and to a lesser degree over pay and employment, user charges for nonbasic services, and investments and the financing thereof (Lieberman et al. 2005).

- Reforms in health insurance have also taken place. Since 2003, a substantial effort has been made through a program known as Decision 139 to extend insurance coverage to the poor and other disadvantaged groups through the use of tax-financed enrollment, with the central government picking up the bulk of the cost, but provincial governments responsible for some cofinancing, identification of beneficiaries, and implementation. Here, too, the tension between central and local governments was evident: central government requested that provinces enroll beneficiaries in the health insurance program, but half of the provinces initially opted instead to pool their Decision 139 allocation with their other resources, exempt beneficiaries from fees at the facility, and reimburse providers directly (Knowles et al. 2005).

• In 2005, several further changes were introduced in Vietnam's health insurance program: the benefit package became more generous, with copayments scrapped; all formal sector workers were required to enroll; the insurer could contract with private providers; in the case of hospital referrals among the poor, transport costs would be covered; and so on.

• Finally, the government, partly with the assistance of international donors including the World Bank, began a program of improving Vietnam's network of primary care facilities. This program appears to have had some impact on utilization of primary care services and their quality, but less than might have been the case had the program's reach extended beyond capital investments to include, for example, demand-side barriers to utilization (Fritzen 2007).

Recent Health Policy Agenda

Yet more changes are planned for Vietnam's health sector for the end of the 2000s. The schedule of user charges, which has not been altered since 1995 and which dictates the amounts providers receive from fee-paying patients and the insurance program, is to be revised upward; some changes have already been made. These changes, it is argued, will help close the now considerable gap between the cost of care and the revenues that providers receive from fee-paying patients and the insurance program. Hospitals that meet certain criteria are to be granted even greater autonomy so as to make them more entrepreneurial and financially self-sufficient. At the same time, however, the government is intent on reducing Vietnam's reliance on out-of-pocket payments, which in 2005 accounted for 68 percent of total health spending.

Its strategy for marrying these apparently contradictory policy thrusts centers largely on the health insurance program. It plans to raise the poverty line below which people would be eligible for free health insurance and to provide subsidies to the near-poor to join the scheme. It is in the final stages of preparing a new health insurance law (promised several years ago) aimed in part at expanding coverage further. Some changes ahead of the new law have already occurred, including rescinding the rule that required informal sector workers and their families to join as a family or as part of a group. The government also plans to increase its capital spending aimed at upgrading health facilities, particularly in poorer areas, in recognition of the fact that while intergovernmental transfers reduce inequalities in fiscal capacity in Vietnam, they do not eliminate them, and as a result, recurrent and capital spending on health is lowest in the poorer parts of Vietnam.

Whether these countervailing measures will be enough to prevent out-of-pocket payments from increasing as user charges are uprated to today's prices, and hospitals are granted still further autonomy, is a matter of debate among commentators. A view held by some is that there are two sets of reforms pulling in different directions: the uprating of the fee schedule and the increased autonomy of providers, which are likely to push the government away from its goal of reducing the systems' reliance on out-of-pocket payments; and the expansion of insurance (especially to those in the bottom half of the income distribution) and the extra government spending on health infrastructure, which are likely to help the government toward its goal.

The depth of concern within the government over health financing issues was underscored by a report on Vietnam's health insurance program released in 2007 by the National Assembly's Committee for Social Affairs. The committee noted that the transfer of responsibility for fund management from provincial to central government in 1995 had produced some perverse incentives: a poor province lacking expensive high-tech equipment would likely run a surplus, which would end up covering the deficit of a rich province spending in excess of its revenues due to its costly high-tech care. The committee noted several other challenges: underenrollment among formal sector workers; adverse selection in the voluntary program; unrealistically low revenues (for example, the 3 percent contribution rate for formal sector workers was argued to be low by international standards); supplier-induced demand caused by the use of fee-for-service payments; and weak and unenforceable contracts between the insurer and providers.

It is against this background that this book has been written. The present time seems an opportune moment to take stock of Vietnam's achievements in the health sector and the challenges it faces, and to offer some ideas as to how the challenges could be met. This is what this book sets out to do, paying special attention to the areas that are currently uppermost in policy makers' minds: health insurance and financing, and health delivery. It builds on analytic work on Vietnam's health system undertaken by Bank staff and consultants, but draws on a number of other sources. These include: analytic work undertaken by the Vietnamese government and Vietnamese scholars; studies commissioned by other international organizations, especially those in the Joint Health Initiative; studies undertaken by the World Bank and others on other sectors and on cross-cutting themes, including the 2008 Vietnam Development Report 2008: Social Protection; and studies by the Bank and others on other countries, both in the region and beyond.

Vietnam's Health System Now

Vietnam spends around 5–6 percent of its GDP on health—the share increased somewhat in the early 2000s, but has since fallen back. Given its per capita income, and the relationship across countries between per capita income and health spending, Vietnam's total health spending (as a share of GDP) is broadly in line with expectations (figure 1.1). GDP itself grew at an annual rate of 7 percent to 8 percent during the 2002–06 period (only China in the East Asia and Pacific region grew faster), with GDP per capita rising to US$723 in 2006 (at official exchange rates).[1] Per capita

Figure 1.1: Vietnam's Total Health Spending in Context

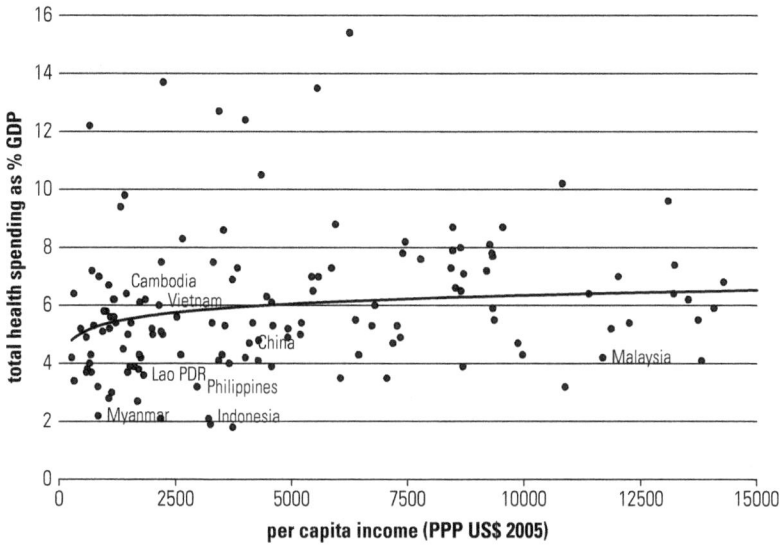

health spending has thus been increasing considerably during this period. The IMF forecasts real GDP growth rates of 8 percent through 2012, despite inflation, which is predicted to peak before the end of the decade. Economic growth is bolstered by rapid export growth, strong foreign and domestic investment, and rising consumption. The likely trend is thus a continued growth of per capita health spending.

Vietnam's health system draws its revenues largely from out-of-pocket payments, which in 2005 accounted for around 70 percent of revenues, up from 60 percent in 1998 (figure 1.2). Over half of these are payments to public providers (classified here following international conventions on national health accounts as private spending, although classified as public spending in Vietnam), one-quarter are for drugs, and the remainder (17 percent) are to private providers, mostly private clinics (figure 1.3). Government health spending (including spending by the social health insurance (SHI) program, whether financed through mandatory or voluntary contributions) accounts for only around one-quarter of health spending, equivalent to around 1.2 percent of GDP.[2] While total health spending in

Figure 1.2: Revenue Sources in Vietnam's Health System, 1998, 2000, and 2005

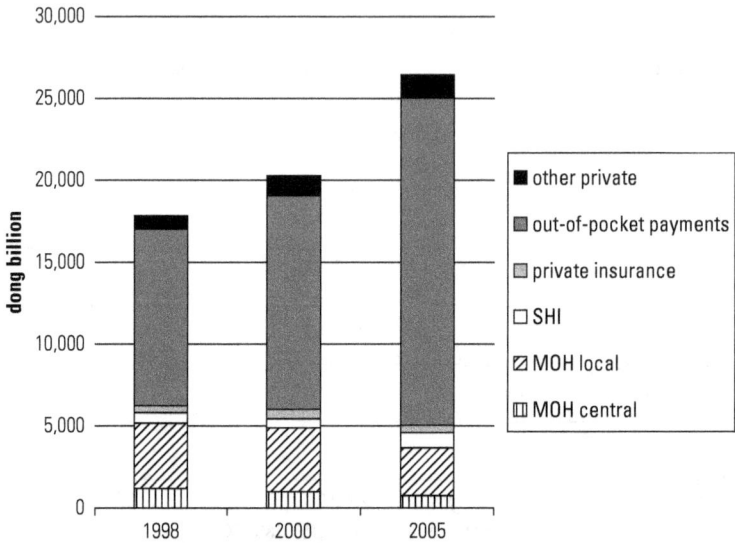

Source: Vietnam National Health Accounts, available from World Health Organization NHA Web site, and Knowles et al.

Figure 1.3: Out-of-Pocket Health Spending, Vietnam 2006

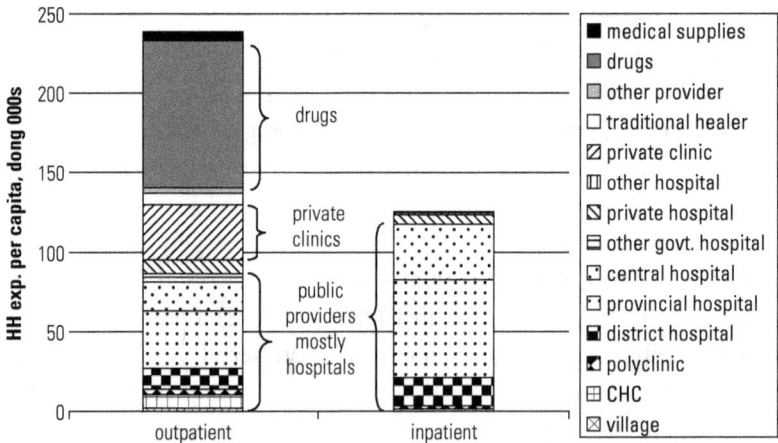

Source: VHLSS 2006.

Vietnam is broadly in line with expectations, Vietnam's government health spending is considerably less than "expected" (figure 1.4). This reflects a relatively small share of government expenditure allocated to the health sector (as figure 1.5 shows, Vietnam's 4 percent to 5 percent compares to an international average among developing

Figure 1.4: Vietnam's Government Health Spending in Context

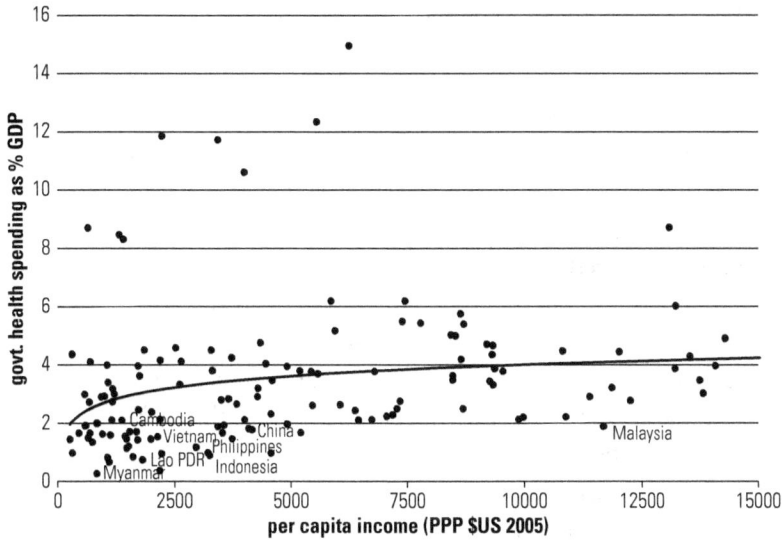

Source: World Development Indicators. Curves are regression lines relating the natural log of the y-axis variable to the natural log of per capita income.

Figure 1.5: Government Health Spending as a Share of Government Spending vs. Total Government Spending as a Share of GDP

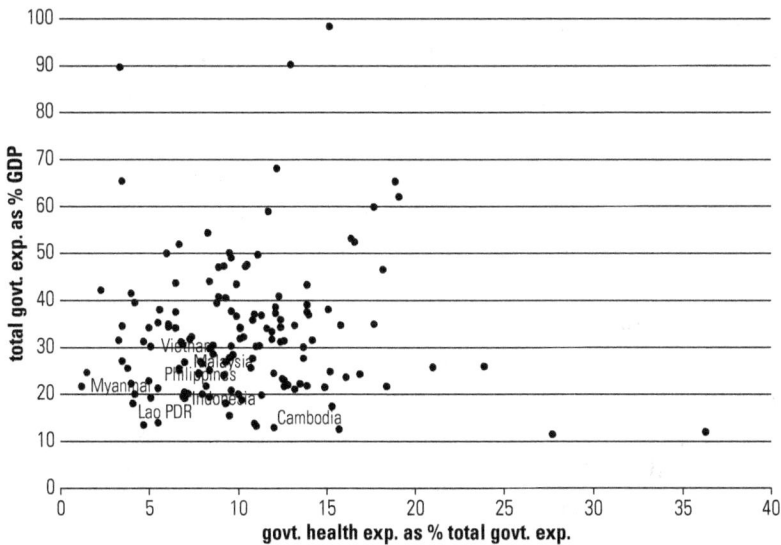

Source: World Development Indicators. Government expenditure.

countries of 10 percent) rather than a small share of government spending in GDP (Vietnam's government spending share of 30 percent is close to the developing country average of 33 percent). There has been some disagreement between IMF staff and the government over whether the government's spending is fiscally sustainable. IMF staff note that the overall fiscal deficit is relatively small (less than 4 percent of GDP), but warned about possible expenditure increases through higher public sector wages and pensions and falling revenues through reductions in oil-related revenues.[3] The government argues, however, that its fiscal deficit is more likely to stay constant, arguing that it has no additional spending plans, that it envisages no extraordinary revenue shortfalls, and that it remains committed to expanding general government revenue sources through a broadening of the tax base.

In Vietnam, the financing and delivery of government programs, including health care, is highly decentralized. As a result, by far the biggest component of government spending is local government (mostly provincial) spending. This raises concerns over interjurisdictional equity, with the fear being that poorer local governments—whose populations are likely to have the greatest health needs—will end up spending less on health. This is indeed the case: The concentration indices for government health spending in figure 1.6 are positive, indicating a pro-rich distribution across Vietnam's eight regions. Interregional inequalities in government health spending are larger than interregional inequalities in overall government spending, but are smaller than interregional inequalities in per capita income. The inequalities favoring richer regions in government spending and government health spending occur despite the pro-poor targeting of transfers for national target programs (NTPs); these include the exemption of education fees for poor households, as well as a consolidated health NTP addressing malaria, TB, and other public health issues. The good news is that the aforementioned innovations in the intergovernmental transfer system introduced in 2004 appear to have reduced interregional inequalities in government spending: The concentration index fell between 2002 and 2004 for general government spending and even more for government health spending (figure 1.6). That said, it should be noted that the

Figure 1.6: Inter-Regional Inequalities in Government Health Spending, 2002 and 2006

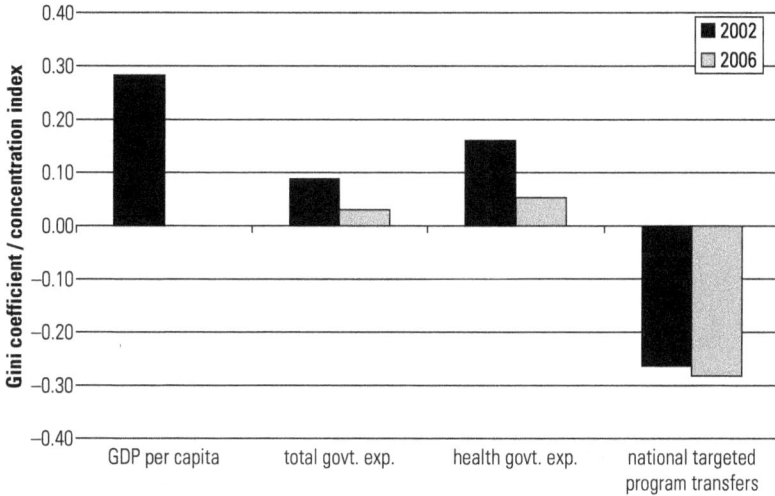

Source: Calculated from financial data from MOF (accessed 15 June 2007). Data for 2002 and 2004 are actual/final accounts. Data for 2006 are planned accounts. Health expenditures for 2002–06 are for recurrent health expenditures only.

Note: The Gini coefficient and concentration index are calculated from population-weighted data on the eight regions.

inequalities in figure 1.6 mask within-province inequalities in Vietnam: Provinces enjoy considerable discretion in how they allocate budgets (including funds from targeted programs) across districts and communes, and there may be considerable inequities between poor and rich parts of a province (World Bank 2005).

Also noteworthy in figure 1.2 is the small (albeit increasing) share of total health spending covered by SHI. The smallness reflects both the limited (albeit rising) coverage rate and the shallowness of coverage. The latter reflects the fact that most out-of-pocket payments are incurred not in government facilities, but rather at drug stores and private facilities that are not covered by the insurance scheme.

What of the pooling function of health financing? In contrast to many countries, Vietnam spends the majority of its government health spending on goods and services rather than salaries, though the share going to salaries has risen in recent years (Government of Vietnam-Donor Working Group on Public Expenditure Review 2000; Knowles et al. 2005). But as in many countries, the bulk of Vietnam's government health spending goes to urban hospitals (75 percent to

87 percent). Unsurprisingly, as a result, it is the better-off who benefit disproportionately from government health spending, though Vietnam fares better in this respect than China, India, and Indonesia (figure 1.7). Pooling has improved in the health insurance scheme, as the fraction of the population covered has risen, thanks largely to the aforementioned health insurance scheme for the poor. By 2004, around 15 percent of the population was covered through this program, and those covered were disproportionately poor (Wagstaff 2007b). By 2006, in total around 40 percent of Vietnamese were covered. Furthermore, in contrast to the situation in some neighboring countries, the benefit package is broadly similar for all enrolled groups. Chapter 3 goes into the health insurance program in some detail, and chapter 4 suggests how it might be reformed.

In terms of provider payment methods, Vietnam operates a mix of budget (for the tax-financed supply-side subsidies) and fee-for-service (FFS). Supply-side subsidies, which are allocated according to planned bed and population numbers, reduce the fees payable by both fee-paying and insured patients. Fees are set by the government, and as mentioned above, are due to be uprated, having been set in 1995. (New technologies are priced at current prices, presenting providers with an incentive to deliver them in preference to old technologies.) Some experimentation with prospective payments has

Figure 1.7: Who Benefits from Government Health Spending in Vietnam?

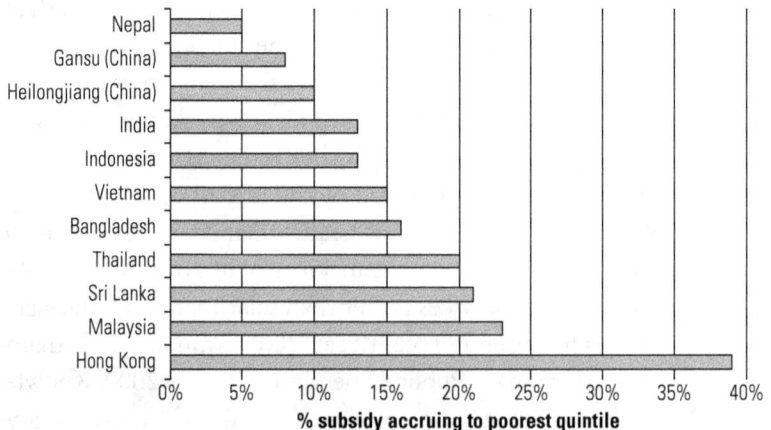

% subsidy accruing to poorest quintile

Source: O'Donnell et al.

occurred, but to date has been very limited. Fees were estimated in 2003 to account for 43 percent of hospital revenues nationwide, though household data suggest the figure may be higher (the discrepancy may be due to informal payments) (World Bank 2005). Chapter 5 discusses provider payments in some detail, and chapter 6 discusses possible reforms.

What of the organization of providers? In the public sector, Vietnam still operates the tiered pyramid model that it developed in the north prior to unification: CHCs sit at the bottom; above them sit intercommune polyclinics; above them district hospitals; then provincial hospitals; and at the very top sit central hospitals and specialty institutes. On average, a CHC serves just 7,000 people—comparable to the figure in Thailand (Government of Vietnam-Donor Working Group on Public Expenditure Review 2000). CHC users, unsurprisingly, are disproportionately poor, while the better-off are disproportionately heavy users of hospitals. Hospital bed occupancy rates are high, especially at the provincial level, as is the inpatient admission rate, which in the 1990s exceeded that of Korea (World Bank 2001). This reflects the tendency of people to bypass lower-level facilities and overuse higher-level facilities, a tendency exacerbated by the incentive that providers have to increase their bed occupancy rates and hence their supply-side subsidies (which are based on bed norms), and the incentive that patients have to use higher-level facilities because the fee difference between low- and high-level facilities is relatively small. As mentioned earlier, the public sector delivery system has been the subject of two major policy initiatives: a major capital program to upgrade facilities—especially those at the bottom of the pyramid—in part in an effort to discourage the bypassing of lower-level facilities; and an autonomization program where higher-level facilities especially have been granted ever more autonomy and have been expected to become increasingly self-sufficient financially. Further information on the public system is contained in chapter 4, which also explores and assesses the government's autonomization program, a subject of some debate currently.

The private sector appears to have grown considerably in recent years, though private providers did exist in the south prior to unification, but data from that period are not available. Drug vendors are the biggest group, though general practitioner clinics are also important; the private hospital sector, by contrast, is highly undeveloped (Government of Vietnam-Donor Working Group on Public Expenditure Review 2000).

Overview of the Chapters

The book begins in chapter 2 with an assessment of recent trends in the performance of Vietnam's health sector, focusing on health outcomes and financial protection. In many respects, Vietnam's performance relative to health outcomes continues to be strong. Between 2000 and 2005, Vietnam saw reductions in age-specific mortality across all ages, in contrast to Thailand, where rates increased at some ages, and Malaysia, where the decline in mortality stagnated. Vietnam's age-specific death rates compare favorably now with those of Malaysia. But trends in some health indicators have been less favorable, and improvements have in general been larger among Vietnam's better-off and in Vietnam's better-off regions. With respect to financial protection Vietnam scores badly (the risk of "catastrophic" health expenditures is high by international standards); furthermore, the improvements of the 1990s do not appear to have been continued into the 2000s.

The book looks at health insurance in chapter 3. It finds that coverage has expanded considerably recently, but argues that this recent growth of coverage will not continue, and that new policy measures beyond those currently being debated will be required to further expand coverage. The book also finds that insurance affords relatively little financial protection in Vietnam, in part because coverage is so shallow, but also because of weak cost control by the health insurance agency. The book goes on in chapter 4 to propose and to estimate the costs of reforms to health insurance that would both expand and deepen coverage. The more ambitious reform would see a shift to a single-payer model, with the health insurer being responsible for the vast majority of total health spending in Vietnam (currently it accounts for just 10 percent). This reform would facilitate the uprating of user fees, and would also involve a shift away from supply-side subsidies toward demand-side subsidies; the latter would further improve equity in government health spending.

Chapters 5 and 6 look at service delivery. Chapter 5 finds that costs in the hospital sector have been rising rapidly, and the cost increases cannot for the most part be explained in terms of higher caseload or a more complex case mix. Rather, they seem to be due to an ever more sophisticated style of care. Whether health status has improved commensurately is not clear. In fact, there is a widespread suspicion that it has not. The report also finds that measures to provide hospitals with greater financial autonomy have probably exacerbated matters, increasing the amount hospitals have charged patients, and pushing up hospital administration costs. Chapter 6 then offers some ideas for reforming service providers. Two key measures include the introduction of clinical guidelines operationalized via clinical pathways, and the reform of the ways providers are paid, switching from fee-for-service to some form of "prospective" system, such as case-based payments for hospitals and capitation payments for lower-level providers. In each case, the reforms would have the biggest "bite" if Vietnam were able to shift to a single-payer model. If it did so, the autonomization reforms already started would make sense to continue. If not, the wisdom of these reforms is unclear.

Finally, chapter 7 examines the role of different parts of government in the health sector, and argues that greater clarity of roles and responsibilities—horizontally and vertically—will be required, especially if the more ambitious reforms are to be pursued.

CHAPTER 2

Recent Trends in Vietnam's Health Sector Performance

Health systems are to be judged ultimately according to how well they improve a population's health. Of course, health systems are not the only things that matter for health outcomes, and it is difficult—if not impossible—to identify the individual contribution that a health system makes to health improvements. Nonetheless, looking at trends in health outcomes—both averages and inequalities, and in an international context—is useful, and some attempts can be made to see how far these can be attributed to the health system. Health systems are, of course, not just about improving health. Good ones also organize the financing of health services in such a way that people are protected from the financial consequences of illness and death.

This chapter starts by looking at recent trends in health outcomes in Vietnam, setting Vietnam's performance in an international context and in the context of its rapid economic growth. It finds that on child mortality Vietnam has done well, even when its performance is adjusted for its recent rapid growth. But on other health indicators Vietnam has done less well: the incidence of fever and acute respiratory infection (ARI) among children increased between 1998 and 2002, while in Indonesia and the Philippines it fell; and Vietnam has lagged behind Cambodia, China, Indonesia, and the Philippines in reducing TB prevalence and mortality. The chapter next examines the evidence on trends in health inequalities. It finds that inequalities in infant and under-five mortality have continued to widen in Vietnam, while in the Philippines and Indonesia they have either narrowed or increased only marginally. Vietnam's richer south and Red River Delta have reduced infant mortality faster than the poorer central and northern regions of the country. Finally, this chapter looks at financial protection, measured in terms of the fraction of households experiencing catastrophic health spending. It finds that Vietnam fares badly by international standards, and its performance has worsened recently, after having improved during the 1990s. It finds that inpatient expenses account for only half of the spending of households experiencing catastrophic spending, with the other half of spending in such households is due to the steady drip-drip-drip of spending on drugs and outpatient visits. Recent increases in the incidence of catastrophic spending have been most pronounced in the southeast and Mekong Delta.

Health Outcomes

One key indicator of population health—and the only indicator for which internationally comparable time-series data are available—is childhood mortality. During the 1980s, Vietnam's performance in reducing under-five mortality was somewhat disappointing, averaging a 2 percent annual reduction during the first half of the 1980s and a 1 percent annual reduction during the second half of the 1980s (figure 2.1). China, Indonesia, the Philippines, and Thailand as a group did better than Vietnam during the 1980s. However, Vietnam's performance—in absolute terms and relative to these other countries—picked up in the early 1990s, and improved further in the late 1990s and the first half of the 2000s. During the period 1995–2000, in fact, Vietnam was ahead of all four countries in its annual rate of under-five mortality reduction, and in the period 2000–05 was beaten only by China.

Of course, it could be argued that Vietnam's recent strong performance on child mortality has nothing to do with the health system, and reflects instead the strong recent growth of per capita income, known to be an important determinant of child mortality (Pritchett and Summers 1996). In fact, it turns out that even after taking into account its strong economic growth, Vietnam still looks like a good performer in terms of child mortality reduction.

Figure 2.1: Vietnam's Under-Five Mortality Trends in Historical and International Context

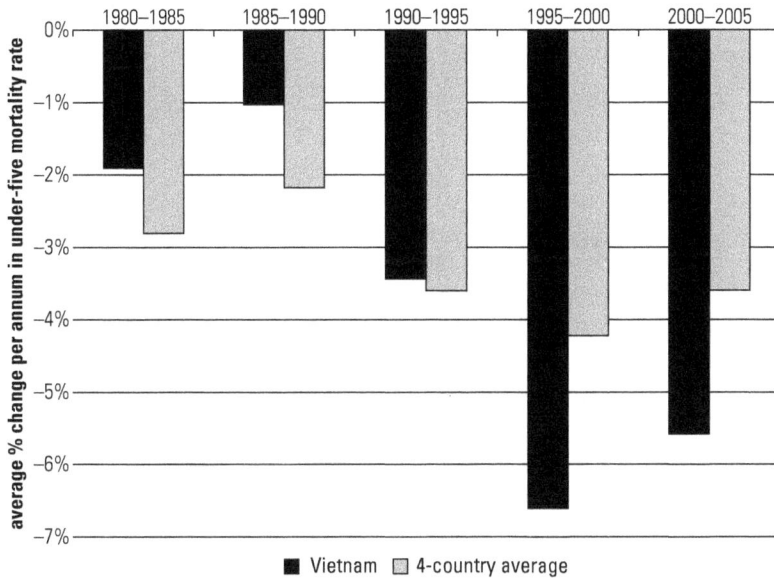

Source: computed from World Bank's World Development Indicators. The four countries included in the four-country average are China, Indonesia, The Philippines, and Thailand.

By running a cross-country regression of five-year percentage changes in under-five mortality (or infant mortality) on rates of per capita income growth and previous periods' values of mortality, one can compute an "expected" rate of change of mortality— the rate of change predicted given the country's economic growth and starting value of mortality (table 2.1). In the late 1980s, Vietnam's performance in terms of mortality reduction fell short of what it might reasonably be expected to have been. In the first half of the 1990s, Vietnam's performance was roughly what might reasonably have been expected. In the late 1990s and first half of the 2000s, in contrast, Vietnam reduced infant and under-five mortality faster than expected on the basis of its economic growth and initial mortality rate.

Child mortality is but one indicator of child health outcomes, albeit an important one. Data on other indicators of child health show Vietnam's recent performance on health outcomes in a less favorable light (figure 2.2). According to the Demographic and Health Survey

Table 2.1: Actual and Expected Annual Rates of Change of Infant and Under-Five Mortality, 1980–2005, by Subperiod

COUNTRY	PERIOD	UNDER-FIVE MORTALITY		INFANT MORTALITY	
		ACTUAL	EXPECTED	ACTUAL	EXPECTED
China	1980–1985	−4.9%	−3.7%	−4.6%	−3.4%
	1985–1990	−0.4%	−3.6%	−0.5%	−3.3%
	1990–1995	−1.3%	−4.0%	−0.5%	−3.7%
	1995–2000	−2.3%	−3.8%	−2.3%	−3.5%
	2000–2005	−5.6%	−4.0%	−4.8%	−3.7%
Indonesia	1980–1985	−2.7%	−2.7%	−2.4%	−2.6%
	1985–1990	−3.6%	−3.0%	−3.1%	−2.8%
	1990–1995	−6.4%	−3.2%	−4.5%	−3.0%
	1995–2000	−6.4%	−2.8%	−5.8%	−2.6%
	2000–2005	−4.5%	−3.4%	−3.9%	−3.1%
Philippines	1980–1985	−1.3%	−2.4%	−1.2%	−2.3%
	1985–1990	−4.1%	−3.0%	−2.7%	−2.9%
	1990–1995	−4.7%	−2.9%	−3.2%	−2.7%
	1995–2000	−4.1%	−3.2%	−3.1%	−3.0%
	2000–2005	−3.0%	−3.4%	−2.9%	−3.2%
Thailand	1980–1985	−5.5%	−3.3%	−3.9%	−3.0%
	1985–1990	−3.5%	−3.9%	−3.5%	−3.6%
	1990–1995	−7.1%	−3.9%	−6.4%	−3.6%
	1995–2000	−3.3%	−3.5%	−3.4%	−3.2%
	2000–2005	−0.7%	−4.0%	−0.9%	−3.7%
Vietnam	1980–1985	−2.9%		−1.9%	
	1985–1990	−1.5%	−3.2%	−1.0%	−3.0%
	1990–1995	−3.7%	−3.6%	−3.4%	−3.3%
	1995–2000	−7.7%	−3.6%	−6.6%	−3.4%
	2000–2005	−5.1%	−4.0%	−5.6%	−3.7%

Source: Computed from World Bank's World Development Indicators.

(DHS), the incidence of diarrhea among children grew between 1997–98 and 2002–03 in Indonesia, the Philippines, and Vietnam, and the increase in Vietnam was not much higher than that in Indonesia and a good deal smaller than that in the Philippines. However, while the rates of incidence of ARI and fever fell or stayed unchanged in Indonesia and the Philippines, they increased in Vietnam by over 5 percentage points.

Figure 2.2: Trends in Childhood Health Indicators, 1997–98 to 2002–03

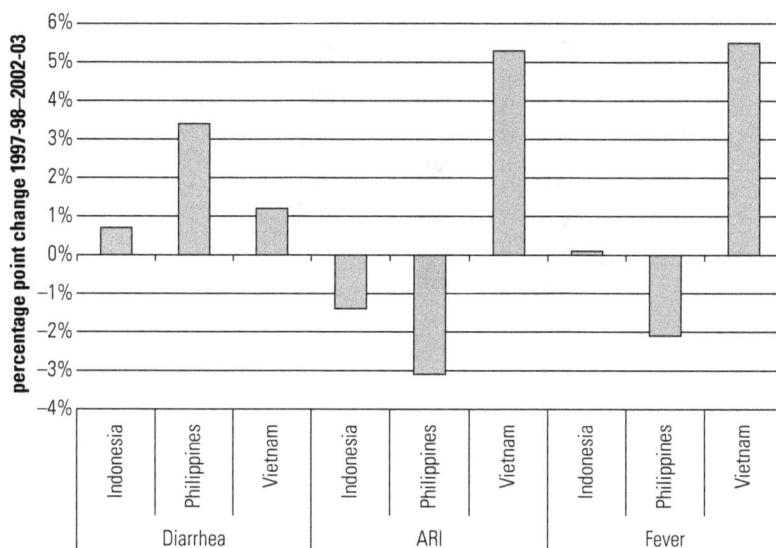

Source: Based on Gwatkin et al.

What of Vietnam's health beyond children? Vietnam's recent trends in TB mortality and prevalence (figure 2.3) present a somewhat worrying picture. On average, for the years 2002–05, only Thailand achieved a lower annual rate of reduction of TB mortality and prevalence than Vietnam. But Vietnam's achievement in age-specific mortality for all causes of death looks rather good (figure 2.4). Unlike Thailand, which saw rising age-specific mortality rates at some ages between 2000 and 2005, and Malaysia, where the decline in age-specific mortality appears to have stagnated, Vietnam saw reductions in age-specific mortality at all ages between 2000 and 2005. Furthermore, by 2005, Vietnam's age-specific death rates compared favorably with those of Malaysia across the full range of ages. For people below the age of 55, Vietnam's rates were a good deal better than those in Thailand.

Policy makers continue to express concern over communicable diseases, but these relate to new and reemerging diseases, including tuberculosis, HIV/AIDS, avian flu, SARS, dengue fever, and Japanese encephalitis. As a group, these likely comprise a rising share of the

Figure 2.3: Trends in TB Mortality and Prevalence

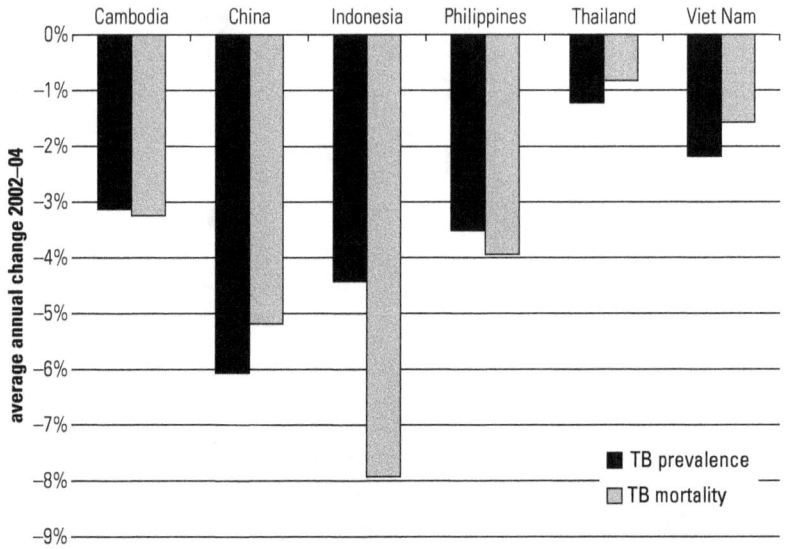

Source: UN Statistical Division Millennium Indicators Database http://unstats.un.org/unsd/mi/mi_goals.asp.

Figure 2.4: Trends in Age-Adjusted Mortality—Vietnam Compared to Malaysia and Thailand

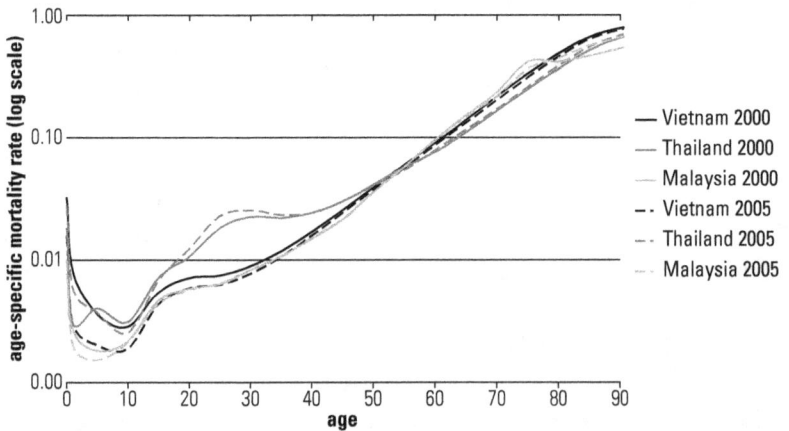

Source: WHO Life Tables for Member States http://www.who.int/whosis/database/life_tables/life_tables.cfm.

burden of disease in Vietnam. And of course each has a devastating potential to cause large numbers of deaths.

Finally, with incidence having leaped and still rising, the most potent threat to health and length of life for most Vietnamese comes from cancer, cardiovascular disease (CVD), diabetes, and mental illness, along with accidents, injuries, and poisoning. These "non-communicable" diseases and conditions (NCDs) already account for nearly 60 percent of all deaths, with this proportion likely to rise in the short to medium term. Their importance is evident even in relatively low-income settings. In the Bavi district in Ha Tay Province, the overall leading causes of death were found to be CVD, malignant neoplasms, and infectious diseases. Accidents and their adverse effects also contributed a large part of mortality, with the leading type of accident being drowning for small children and traffic-related accidents for young men. In terms of premature mortality, CVD, malignant neoplasms, accidents, natural disasters and other external causes were also leading causes. Moreover, the contribution to premature mortality of perinatal causes, injuries from various sources, and malignant neoplasms exceeded their role in overall mortality. Control or prevention efforts in respect to each of these causes is thus indicated. Each entails technical and organizational interventions and behavioral adjustments so distinctive as to make joint policy responses the exception rather than the norm. Similarly, success in tackling the NCDs, as with the new and resurgent communicable diseases, requires policies that respond to the often highly distinctive technical, organizational, and behavioral features of each problem.

Health Inequalities

While Vietnam seems to have done reasonably well in terms of *average* levels of health (at least according to some indicators), it seems to have done less well in terms of addressing health inequalities between the poor and better-off. Figure 2.5 shows how infant mortality has fallen faster in Vietnam's richer southern regions, and least quickly in its poorer northern regions. Inequalities across wealth groups also seem

Figure 2.5: Faster Infant Mortality Reduction in Vietnam's Richer South

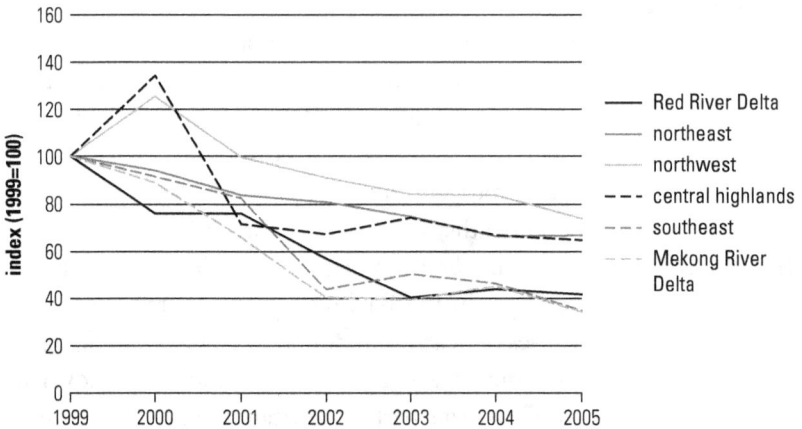

Source: Vietnam Health Yearbook.

to have been widening. A 2003 study of trends in child mortality inequalities based on data from the 10 years preceding the 1992–93 and 1997–98 Vietnam Living Standards Surveys warned of a growing gap in child survival prospects between the poor and better-off (Wagstaff and Nguyen 2003). A more recent study using data from the 10 years preceding the 1997 and 2002 Demographic and Health Surveys points to a continuation of this trend (Gwatkin et al. 2003). Figure 2.6 shows the changes in inequality in infant and under-five mortality for Vietnam, and for the Philippines and Indonesia over the same period. The vertical axis is the concentration index, and a negative value indicates a concentration of deaths among the poorer section of the wealth distribution.[4] Despite the rise in inequality in child mortality between 1992–93 and 1997–98 in Vietnam, the Philippines, and Indonesia, in 1997–98 both the Philippines and Indonesia had larger poor-nonpoor gaps in infant and under-five mortality than Vietnam. By 2002–03, this picture had been reversed; between 1998 and 2002–03, Indonesia cut its inequality in child mortality, and the Philippines experienced a smaller increase in inequality than Vietnam.[5]

Table 2.2, using data from the same study (Gwatkin et al. 2003), digs further into this question of widening gaps in child mortality in Vietnam. The largest percentage reductions in both infant and under-five mortality in Vietnam over the period 1997–2002 occurred

Figure 2.6: Trends in Inequality in Infant and Under-Five Mortality, Vietnam, Philippines, and Indonesia

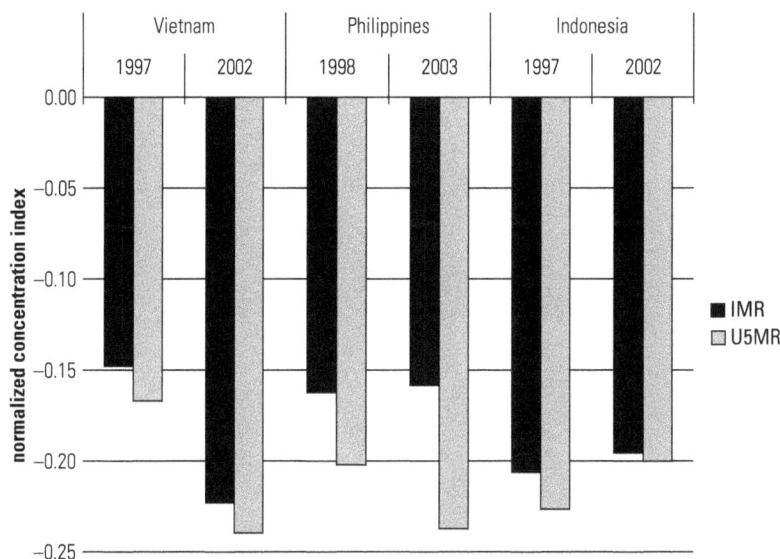

Source: Based on Gwatkin et al.

among the third and fourth wealth quintiles. The poorest fifth of the population saw the smallest percentage reductions. The table also shows that inequalities in childhood immunization coverage grew over this period, with the poorest fifth of the population barely seeing any rise in the fraction of children fully immunized. The richest fifth of Vietnamese children, in contrast, saw a 55 percent increase. Inequalities grew, too, in the prevalence of childhood illnesses. The prevalence of fever increased across all wealth groups, but the poorest fifth experienced an increase that was nearly twice that of the population as a whole. The prevalence of diarrhea fell among the top two wealth groups and rose among the poorest two groups: the poorest group experienced the largest increase, and the richest fifth experienced the largest reduction. Differences across wealth groups in trends in the prevalence of ARI are less clear-cut, but the poorest group saw a bigger increase than the richest group.

Arguably more interesting are trends in inequalities in the *treatment* of childhood illness. Table 2.2 shows that in terms of *whether*

Table 2.2: Percentage Changes in Childhood Health Indicators, Vietnam 1997–2002, by Wealth Quintile

| INDICATOR | DESCRIPTION | WEALTH QUINTILES | | | | | POP AVERAGE |
		LOWEST	SECOND	MIDDLE	FOURTH	HIGHEST	
Child mortality							
Infant mortality rate	Deaths under age 12 months per 1,000 live births	-8%	-36%	-44%	-44%	-18%	-29%
Under-five mortality rate	Deaths under 5 years per 1,000 live births	-16%	-26%	-44%	-42%	-31%	-28%
Childhood immunization							
BCG coverage	% of children age 12–23 months who have	3%	13%	-2%	2%	3%	4%
Measles coverage	% of children age 12–23 months who have received measles vaccination	0%	11%	8%	4%	11%	8%
DPT coverage	% of children age 12–23 months who have received DPT vaccination	-4%	-5%	23%	22%	15%	10%
Full basic vaccination coverage	% of children age 12–23 months who have received BCG, measles, and DPT	5%	20%	47%	36%	54%	33%
Childhood illness							
Prevalence of fever	% ill in the preceding 2 weeks	49%	27%	9%	24%	22%	26%
Prevalence of diarrhea	% ill in the preceding 2 weeks	80%	11%	1%	-23%	-39%	12%
Prevalence of acute respiratory infection	% ill in the preceding 2 weeks	69%	18%	23%	72%	39%	37%

Treatment of childhood illness

Medical treatment of fever	% seen medically if ill	19%	12%	1%	14%	35%	15%
Treatment of fever in a public facility	% seen in public facility if ill	56%	-24%	-1%	-38%	-28%	-6%
Treatment of fever in a private facility	% seen in private facility if ill	-29%	70%	2%	144%	103%	41%
Medical treatment of ARI	% seen medically if ill	18%	12%	-6%	-13%	-3%	3%
Treatment of ARI in a public facility	% seen in public facility if ill	70%	-18%	-2%	-52%	-57%	-10%
Treatment of ARI in a private facility	% seen in private facility if ill	-47%	53%	-10%	78%	92%	17%

Source: Gwatkin et al.

sick children receive treatment for fever and ARI, there are no clear trends; in fact, in the case of ARI, the probability of a sick child being treated increased among the poor, but fell among the better-off. What does come through clearly, however, is a growth of inequality in *where* sick children are treated. The probability of a child suffering from fever or ARI being treated in a public facility increased among poor families, but fell among better-off families. The opposite was true of private facilities, with a sharp substitution toward private facilities in the treatment of fever and ARI among better-off households.

Growing regional differences emerge in other indicators, as well, with differentiating factors including variations within the country in exposure to traditional diseases and health problems. Child malnutrition and the traditional communicable diseases remain serious public health concerns in poor upland areas. In most other areas, however, the incidence of traditional infectious diseases has fallen sharply in the last 30 years—from 58.5 percent in 1976 to 19 percent in 2003.

Financial Protection

Health systems are, as mentioned at the beginning of the chapter, not just about improving health. Good ones also organize the financing of health services in such a way that people are protected from the financial consequences of illness and death. By international standards, Vietnam's health system does not fare terribly well in respect to financial protection, at least as far as the direct (out-of-pocket) expenses associated with illness are concerned.[6] Furthermore, its performance does not seem to have improved in the 2000s.

In 1997–98, over 15 percent of the Vietnamese population recorded out-of-pocket health expenses that exceeded 25 percent of their discretionary income (measured by their nonfood consumption; see figure 2.7). Over 5 percent of the population recorded health spending that pushed them above the 40 percent threshold. Of the countries in East Asia for which there are data, only China comes close to recording such high rates of catastrophic out-of-pocket health spending. Out-of-pocket expenses in this study—and the

Figure 2.7: Catastrophic Household Health Expenses, Vietnam and Other East Asian Countries

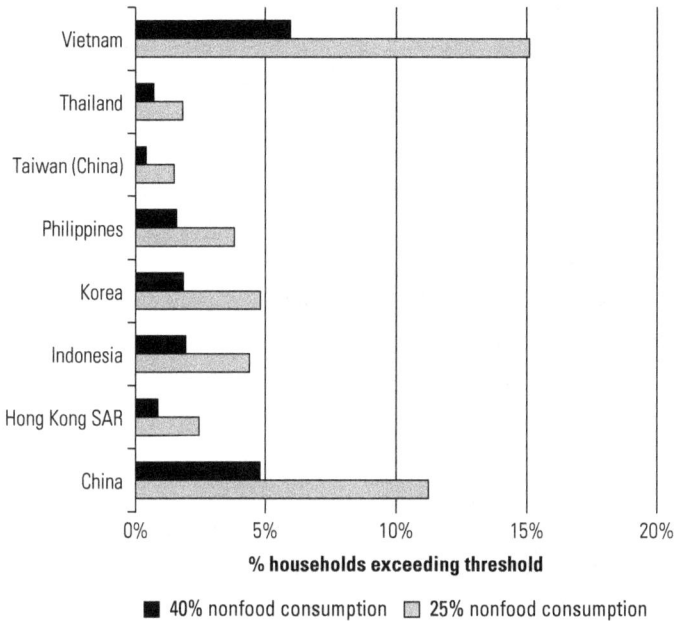

% households exceeding threshold

■ 40% nonfood consumption   ▢ 25% nonfood consumption

Source: Van Doorslaer, O'Donnell, et al.

others discussed below—include payments for drugs and medical supplies, as well as fees paid to providers; they also include formal payments to providers as well as informal (illegal) ones. How large the latter are in Vietnam is unclear (Knowles et al. 2005). The 2002 National Health Survey (NHS) asked people about cash and in-kind "gifts" to providers; surprisingly, only 3 percent of household out-of-pocket spending went to gifts. This figure falls far short of the discrepancy between the amount public providers report as their income from user fees, and the amount respondents in other household surveys say they pay public providers. This may be due to underreporting of gifts in the NHS (for example, confusion between formal and informal fees) or to a lack of distinction in the other household surveys between spending on fees and spending on drugs and other medical items.

How far is inpatient spending responsible for catastrophic health spending? It turns out that spending on inpatient care accounts for only one-half of out-of-pocket spending among those reporting catastrophic health spending (figure 2.8). Spending on outpatient care and medicines accounts for the rest. This is consistent with recent research conducted in the Bavi district of Ha Tay Province, which found that the spending associated with communicable diseases accounts for high health spending among those experiencing catastrophic out-of-pocket expenses, and not one-off calamitous health events such as injuries and hospitalization for noncommunicable diseases (Thuan et al. 2006).

Another way of measuring financial protection is to ask whether out-of-pocket spending makes the difference between a household being above or below the poverty line. The idea is that a poor household with sufficiently large out-of-pocket spending could, in the absence of the health event that necessitated the spending, use the resources to buy enough extra food, clothes, and so forth, and result in its nonmedical consumption being above the poverty line (Wagstaff and van Doorslaer 2003). With this yardstick, too, Vietnam's performance is less than stellar. The poverty head count in Vietnam would have been 1.1 percentage points lower in the absence of out-of-pocket health expenses (Van Doorslaer et al. 2006). This figure is higher than that of Indonesia (0.7), Malaysia (0.1), the Philippines (0.6), and Thailand (0.2), although lower than that of China (2.6). Research

Figure 2.8: Spending Breakdown among Households with Catastrophic Health Spending

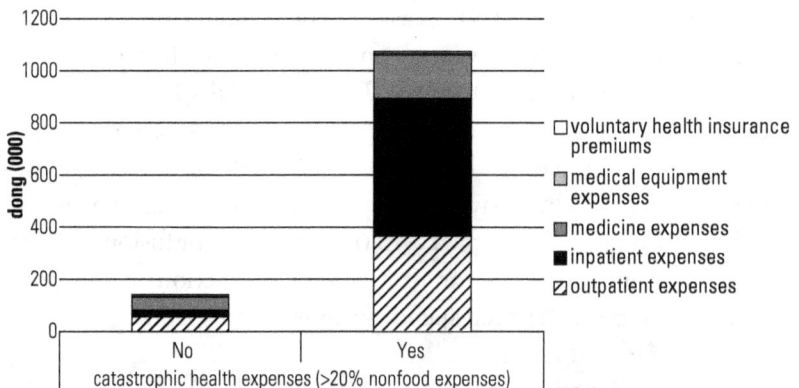

Source: VHLSS 2004.

finds that it is nonhospital spending that is more likely to be impoverishing than hospital spending (Wagstaff and van Doorslaer 2003).

How has Vietnam's performance in terms of financial protection changed over time? Figure 2.9 shows, for a given threshold defined in terms of nonfood expenditure (discretionary income), the fraction of the population with out-of-pocket health expenses that exceed the threshold. So, for example, in 1993, just over 25 percent of the population recorded out-of-pocket expenses in excess of 20 percent of nonfood expenditure. By 1998, only 20 percent of the population had spending above this threshold. A chart like figure 2.9 has merit in that one can see how far one's conclusions about trends in catastrophic health spending depend on the choice of threshold. In this case, *whatever the threshold chosen*, fewer people recorded catastrophic health spending in 1998 than in 1993: the 1998 catastrophic health expenses curve is always below the 1993 curve. Between 1998 and 2002, the incidence of catastrophic health spending also fell—again, independently of which threshold one

Figure 2.9: Trends in Catastrophic Household Health Spending, Vietnam 1993–2006

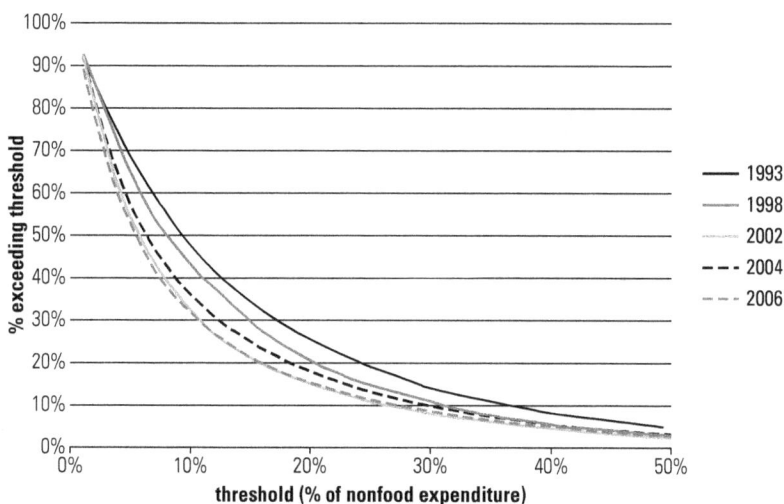

Notes: Calculations from 1992–93 and 1997–98 VLSS surveys, and 2002, 2004, and 2006 VHLSS surveys. Values are weighted to reflect differences in household size and sample weights. For a given threshold of a percentage of nonfood consumption, the height of the curve shows the percentage of households with health spending exceeding the threshold. For example, in 1993, nearly 50% of the population had health care costs exceeding 10% of nonfood consumption.

uses to define catastrophic. Then between 2002 and 2004, the trend was apparently reversed: the curve moved upward over these two years, and the incidence of catastrophic payments increased.[7] This worsening may, however, be a statistical illusion—the 2006 curve is virtually identical to that of 2002. What this also suggests is that there may not have been much of an improvement in financial protection between 2002 and 2006.

CHAPTER 3

Health Insurance

In 1993, four years after the introduction of user fees under *Doi Moi*, the government launched a health insurance program, concerned that user fees would deter people from obtaining care they needed and causing financial hardship to those who did use services. The government's plan is that the formal insurance scheme will gradually replace the free "health card" or "health certificate" that, at least in principle, entitles the holder to free (or subsidized) health care, but which in practice is believed to have worked less well than hoped. The government is, in fact, committed to a goal of universal health insurance (UHI), although it no longer aspires to achieve this by 2010.

How far is the government down the road toward UHI? Will it actually achieve UHI with current policies? Has insurance broadened access to health care as planned, and has it reduced the risk of catastrophic health spending? Is the program financially sustainable? If not, what are the reasons for the program's deteriorating finances? What roles do adverse selection and moral hazard play?

This chapter finds that insurance coverage expansion has increased over the years, and has risen rapidly recently with the launch of a tax-financed program for the poor. There are, however, substantial numbers of people in each target group who have no coverage—not even a health card. The groups that are relatively easy to identify for tax-financed support are already largely covered, while those who are relatively easy to coerce into contributing are mostly contributing. Noncoverage is most pronounced among harder-to-identify and harder-to-coerce groups. The pace of expansion seen in recent years will not continue, and coverage expansion is likely to return to its former slow pace. Insurance has increased utilization of services, but has had only a modest effect on out-of-pocket spending. This reflects in part the fact that the insurer reimburses only a part of the provider's costs, with the rest being covered by supply-side subsidies and out-of-pocket payments. But it also reflects the fact that an important item of household spending on health—namely, drugs bought over the counter—is not covered by insurance. As regards financial sustainability, the last few years have seen a surplus become a deficit, with no signs of a turn-around. Adverse selection and moral hazard are both likely to be contributory factors.

Schemes and Target Groups

Formally, Vietnam has two insurance schemes—a compulsory scheme and a voluntary scheme—though the labels are rather misleading.

- The compulsory scheme includes two subschemes:

  (i) A mandatory earnings-related, contribution-based social health insurance (SHI) scheme for **formal sector workers and civil servants**. Family members are not covered. In the private sector, initially only large companies were required to enroll their workers; now all are. The scheme is run by Vietnam Social Security.

  (ii) A noncontributory scheme, also run by VSS, initially aimed at retired government officials, war veterans, members of Parliament, Communist Party officials, war heroes, and other "people of merit." Subsequently, this group of so-called **policy beneficiaries** was broadened to include children under the age of 6. From 2003 onward, following Decision 139, a noncontributory scheme for **the poor** was added. (The scheme actually covers not only those officially classified as poor, but also ethnic minority households living in remote mountainous areas and households living in communes officially classified as "poor.") Provincial governments are required to contribute to the cost of enrolling under-six children and Decision 139 beneficiaries, and have the option of (though are discouraged from) issuing health cards rather than enrolling beneficiaries in the insurance scheme.

• The "voluntary" scheme has various target groups and associated modalities:

   (i) Full-time **students** are a key target group, and in practice are enrolled en masse by insurance agents operating at their schools or colleges. Premiums are paid by the student's family, and typically there is little that is voluntary about the enroll-ment process. VSS provides insurance for schoolchildren, but so too do other organizations, the largest being Bao Viet, a large multipurpose insurer, specializing originally in shipping.

   (ii) **Family members of the compulsorily insured** can enroll in the VSS voluntary scheme of their own accord, but until recently were required to enroll all household members together. This was to reduce adverse selection. This stipula-tion was scrapped in December 2007.

   (iii) **Others** are allowed by VSS to enroll through group organ-izations, including communes. To reduce adverse selection, 20 percent of the group had been required to register—individuals could not enroll by themselves. This stipulation was scrapped in December 2007. (Private insurance—other than for full-time students—is negligible in Vietnam.)

Contribution Rules, Benefit Packages, Provider Arrangements

Rules concerning financing are summarized in table 3.1. The contribution rate for formal sector workers and civil servants has been 3 percent of earnings for some time, and is split between the employee (1 percent) and employer (2 percent). The contribution of policy beneficiaries is calculated at 3 percent of the minimum

Table 3.1: Finance and Benefit Rules for Health Insurance Programs

PROGRAM	CONTRIBUTIONS	VARIATIONS ON BENEFIT PACKAGE
Compulsory program		
Pensioners	3% of monthly allowances, paid by VSS with subsidies from state budget.	
Meritorious persons, etc.	3% of minimum wage, paid from state budget.	No limits or very generous coverage of services costing more than dong 7 million.
Formal sector workers and civil servants	3% salary, 1% paid by worker, 2% by employer.	
Insurance for the Poor	Dong 50,000, paid out of state budget.	Transport costs for referrals included.
Voluntary program		
Students	Dong 40,000–70,000 (urban). Dong 30,000–50,000 (rural). Paid by parents. In December 2007, the urban contribution was raised to dong 120,000, and the rural contribution to dong 100,000.	
Others	Dong 100,000–160,000 (urban). Dong 70,000–120,000 (rural). Paid by enrollee. In December 2007, the urban contribution was raised to dong 320,000, and the rural contribution to dong 240,000. Subsidy for near-poor; currently 30%, proposed to increase to 70%.	

Source: Interministerial circulars 21/2005/TTLT-BYT-BTC and 22/2005/TTLT-BYT-BTC.

wage, and is paid out of the state budget at the local level. Provinces receive a 100 percent subsidy from the central government to cover the cost of Decision 139 beneficiaries.

The benefit package is essentially the same for everyone. Variations are indicated in table 3.1. The benefit package covers most outpatient and inpatient care received at government facilities; exclusions include interventions covered by vertical programs such as HIV/AIDS prevention and treatment programs, drugs not on the MOH list, treatments not yet approved by MOH, various "luxury" interventions such as cosmetic surgery, dental care, treatment of self-inflicted injuries, and treatment for drug addiction.[8]

Initially when the insurance program was set up, there was no cost sharing. In 2002, cost sharing was introduced, with a 20 percent coinsurance rate but no deductible. In 2005, however, the 20 percent coinsurance rate was scrapped, and cost sharing was applied only on services costing more than D 7 million (US$438). The government is currently toying with the idea of reintroducing the 20 percent coinsurance rate. *It is important to grasp that zero cost sharing does not imply zero out-of-pocket payments.* The cost sharing is defined only over the portion of the cost that VSS is liable for, which is not the full cost of care. Providers bill VSS the fees that are allowed by the fee schedule, as well as an amount for drug costs. The fee schedule was set in 1995 and has not been adjusted (or even uprated in line with inflation), although items have been added to it (at prevailing prices). The result is that VSS picks up only a part of the cost of care. At the health system level, VSS accounts for only 13 percent of total health spending in Vietnam. The rest is accounted for by supply-side subsidies, which account for 20 percent of health expenditures in Vietnam, and out-of-pocket payments, which account for 67 percent of total health spending.

VSS reimburses approved facilities, which include contracted private facilities. Enrollees may also use noncontracted facilities, including providers abroad, but reimbursement in this case is to the patient, who pays the facility and subsequently files a claim, and is limited, in the case of domestic facilities, to the costs incurred on average by public facilities, and in the case of providers abroad to costs incurred on average by central government facilities in Ho Chi Minh City and Hanoi. Enrollees are required to register with a local facility (not necessarily a primary care facility) and are expected to use that facility when they require treatment. Referrals are sanctioned when the registered facility lacks the necessary expertise to treat the patient's condition. VSS normally reimburses facilities via fee for service. VSS may use capitation, however, instead of FFS; the rules concerning the capitation payment are set out in the relevant government circulars.

Coverage

The coverage rates of the various schemes have increased over the years. However, even now—nearly 15 years after the launch of the program—the majority of the population is still uncovered (figure 3.1). There has been steady growth among formal sector workers and schoolchildren, and a dramatic increase in recent years among the poor. Voluntary enrollment among the nonstudent population has stayed low and shows no signs of growing. Given present trends, Vietnam is most unlikely to achieve universal health insurance by 2010, as originally planned.

A better sense of what is constraining the growth of coverage can be obtained by looking at enrollment across different target groups. The various target groups are, of course, not mutually exclusive. We have assumed that the Decision 139 program would want to provide coverage for those who are eligible for it, irrespective of their other characteristics (for example, an under-six child, being in school.). We have assumed that the under-six program would want to provide coverage for all under-six children not eligible for Decision 139,

Figure 3.1: Trends in Insurance Coverage through VSS, Vietnam 1993–2006

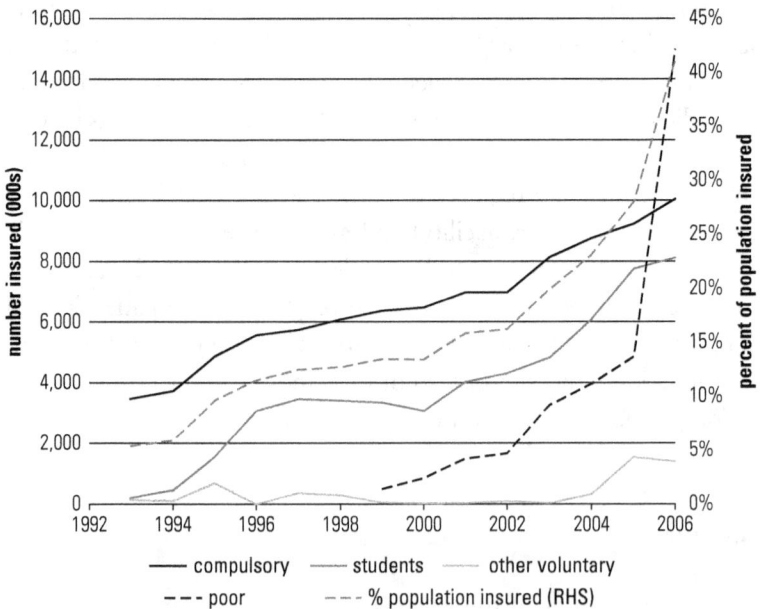

Source: Vietnam Social Security.

even if they are in full-time education or in a family where an adult is insured through the mandatory contributory program for formal sector workers. We have also assumed that the student program would want to cover all full-time students (not part-time students) over the age of 6, unless they are eligible for Decision 139 coverage, and even if they belong to a household where an adult is in the contributory scheme for formal sector workers. Figure 3.2 shows the enrollment numbers for 2006 based on these assumptions. Key points include the following:

- Of Vietnam's 7.7 million **formal sector workers** (just under 10 percent of Vietnam's population of 82 million), 4.8 million (63 percent) are in the contributory scheme, as they ought to be.[9] Another half a million have coverage through one of the other schemes. Two million formal sector workers, however, have no cover of any type. VSS coverage rates among formal sector

Figure 3.2: Enrollment Numbers by Target Group, 2006

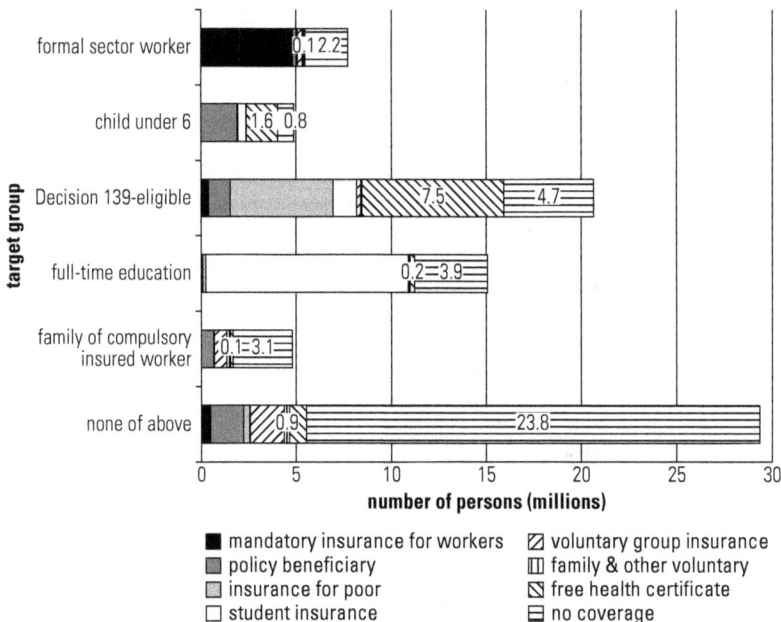

Source: Authors' calculations from 2006 Vietnam Household and Living Standards Survey.

workers are lowest in the home help, construction, motor vehicles, and catering sectors, and highest in the education, health, science and technology, and government sectors (figure 3.3).[10] In some sectors, workers are enrolled in schemes other than the formal sector scheme.

- Vietnam currently has just under 5 million **children ages six or under** who are not eligible for cover under Decision 139. Fewer than 2 million of these are enrolled in the insurance program as policy beneficiaries. Around 400,000 are enrolled in the (voluntary) student program, and a further 1.6 million have a health card. However, almost 1 million under-six children (nearly 20 percent) have no coverage.

- Just over 20 million people in Vietnam (one-quarter of the population) are entitled to cover at the taxpayers' expense through Decision 139, through the **Health Care Fund for the Poor**

Figure 3.3: Enrollment of Formal Sector Workers, by Sector, 2006

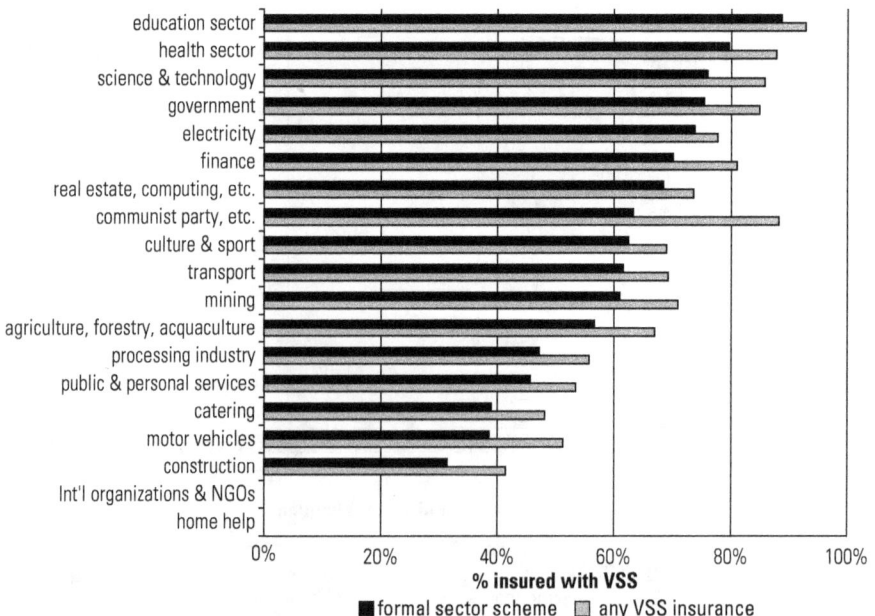

Source: Authors' calculations from 2006 Vietnam Household and Living Standards Survey.

program. Studies show that these people are, as intended, disproportionately poor, despite the fact that eligibility is not based exclusively on poverty status (Wagstaff 2007b). In practice, only 5 million of those entitled to coverage under Decision 139 say they have insurance coverage through the scheme—a much smaller figure than that coming from the official VSS data (14 million). This may reflect confusion among respondents in the household survey about their coverage. A grossed-up figure of just over 1 million people in the sample who are eligible for Decision 139 coverage say they have insurance coverage as a policy beneficiary. Some may in reality be in the Insurance for the Poor program. A large number (7.5 million) of Decision 139 beneficiaries say they have a health certificate. It seems less likely that they are enrolled in the insurance scheme, but it is possible that some of them are. It is also possible that the VSS figure is an estimate, and based on an overly optimistic assumption about the likelihood of provinces enrolling Decision 139 beneficiaries in the insurance scheme rather than giving them a health card. Nearly 5 million of those eligible for coverage under Decision 139 (one-quarter of the total) do not yet have coverage under any scheme.

- Vietnam has around 15 million full-time **students**, just under 20 percent of the population. Nearly 11 million of them have student insurance coverage—30 percent with Bao Viet and other agencies rather than VSS. Another half-million have coverage through one of the other VSS schemes. Nearly 4 million students in Vietnam (one-quarter of the total) currently have no coverage.

- There are around 5 million **family members of formal sector workers** who are not entitled to coverage under Decision 139 or the under-six program, or through full-time education. Currently, less than 1 million of them (18 percent) are enrolled in the voluntary program. A few have coverage through another program, but 3 million people in this category have no coverage.

- The largest population group comprises **people who fall into none of the target groups**. They total nearly 30 million people,

36 percent of Vietnam's population. Just over 15 percent of these people have formal insurance coverage, though 3 percent have a health card. In this category, 24 million people lack coverage of any type. They account for over 60 percent of Vietnam's uninsured population.

Insurance, Access to Health Services, and Financial Protection

How far has insurance increased the use of needed services, as intended? And how far has it helped protect people against the medical care costs associated with ill health?

A number of regression studies have been undertaken that look at the effects of insurance in Vietnam; mostly they use methods that try to eliminate any biases in the estimated insurance coefficient arising from the insurance status variable being correlated with unobservable factors that are also correlated with the outcomes of interest (that is, the problem of health insurance being endogenous) (Trivedi 2003; Jowett et al. 2004; Wagstaff and Pradhan 2005; Sepehri et al. 2006b). These studies find that insurance increases the probability of admission to the hospital and length of stay, as well as (albeit to a lesser extent) the use of outpatient care. They also find evidence of insurance encouraging substitution away from the private sector (including pharmacies) toward the public sector, reflecting the fact that even now the scheme provides coverage largely for care received in public facilities. In the scheme for the poor, insurance has had a bigger impact on the use of inpatient care than outpatient care. Impacts appear to vary across the schemes: for example, the effect of insurance on the probability of admission to the hospital is larger for the formal sector worker scheme than for the scheme for the poor, and smaller still for those in the voluntary scheme (Sepehri et al. 2006b). There is also evidence of impacts varying with income. Membership in the mandatory scheme increases the likelihood of hospital admission for all income groups, but the effect is most pronounced for the middle-income groups. Among the lower income groups, mandatory insurance has no significant impact on length of stay (Sepehri et al. 2006b). In the scheme for the poor, no significant impacts on inpatient care are evident among the poorest 10 percent of the population (Wagstaff 2007b). The lack of impacts among the poor likely reflect the non-price barriers the poor incur in using health services—notably, the transport and time costs.

A simple regression analysis that does not account for the endogeneity of insurance, based on the latest household survey data (the 2006 Vietnam Household Living Standards Survey), suggests that insurance increases the number of outpatient visits and inpatient admissions (table 3.2). It also points to insurance reducing the amount people pay out of pocket per contact (outpatient visit and inpatient admission). In contrast, insurance apparently has no effect on out-of-pocket spending on drugs, and seems to increase the amount that people spend on medical equipment (although the base amount is very small). The results in table 3.2 suggest that, on balance, insurance lowers out-of-pocket payments—the higher costs caused by extra utilization are not enough to outweigh the lower costs per contact. However, the reduction in out-of-pocket spending attributable to insurance is relatively modest (25 percent). Table 3.2 also suggests that insurance reduces the financial risk that people incur, especially large amounts of spending over the year, although again the effect is small—a reduction in the risk of catastrophic spending of 1 percent to 3 percent.

The finding in table 3.2 that insurance has only a modest effect on out-of-pocket spending is broadly consistent with previous studies. Most find a limited impact of insurance on out-of-pocket payments, with the exception being a study of the voluntary program in Hai Phong (Jowett et al. 2003), which found a very large impact. Two studies (Wagstaff and Pradhan 2005; Sepehri et al. 2006a) find an impact in the range -20 percent to -35 percent, and another (Trivedi 2003) found a zero impact. A recent study of the scheme for the poor (Wagstaff 2007b) also found a zero effect. Studies (O'Donnell et al. 2005; Wagstaff 2007b) also have found that insurance in Vietnam has reduced the incidence of catastrophic health spending, but not dramatically. The scheme for the poor, for example, is estimated to have reduced the incidence of catastrophic health spending (spending

Table 3.2: Effects of Insurance on Utilization and Out-of-Pocket Spending, 2006

	HEALTH INSURANCE	FREE HEALTH CARD
No. outpatient visits (% change)	0.244***	0.419***
Out-of-pocket payments per outpatient visit (dong 000s)	−168.601***	−75.175
Out-of-pocket payments for outpatient care (% change)	−0.295***	0.027
No. inpatient admissions (% change)	0.488***	0.636***
Out-of-pocket payments per inpatient admission (dong 000s)	−1266.324***	−699.704***
Out-of-pocket payments for inpatient care (% change)	−0.346***	0.159
Out-of-pocket payments on drugs (% change)	−0.077	−0.121**
Out-of-pocket payments on medical equipment (% change)	0.334***	0.891*
Out-of-pocket payments over last 12 months (% change)	−0.253***	0.071
Out-of-pocket payments exceeding 10% of nonfood consumption (% change)	−0.026***	−0.007
Out-of-pocket payments exceeding 25% of nonfood consumption (% change)	−0.014***	−0.012***

Notes: * $p < .1$, ** $p < .05$, *** $p < .01$. All variables refer to previous 12 months. Spending variables are in thousands of dong. Numbers show effect of insurance on variable indicated, holding constant other influences on the variable in question. Regression equations include, in addition to insurance and possession of a health card, gender, age, region, consumption quintile, illness during the last 4 weeks, and illness during the last 12 months. Equations for the number of contacts and out-of-pocket payments are Poisson models, a model that has been widely used for count data but has also been found to be well suited to modeling out-of-pocket payments. Probit models used for catastrophic spending. Note that these results do not take into account the endogeneity of health insurance.

in excess of 10 percent of nonfood consumption by 3 to 5 percentage points (Wagstaff 2007b). But this still leaves 30 percent *of insured households* incurring catastrophic health spending.

The muted effects of insurance on out-of-pocket payments reflect in part the extra utilization caused by insurance, but also the fact that, as mentioned earlier, VSS does not cover the full cost of care; supply-side subsidies help keep out-of-pocket payments down, but are not enough to eliminate them. It also reflects the fact that much of the out-of-pocket spending in Vietnam is on over-the-counter drugs, and that insurance covers only drugs used during inpatient treatment, and even then only drugs on the MOH list. Some spending is also on private providers, and this spending is typically not reimbursable. This points to another challenge facing the government, in addition to that of expanding coverage: namely, to deepen coverage by reducing copayments and expanding the benefit package, so that insurance exerts a larger downward effect on out-of-pocket spending. Discouragement of unnecessary use of drugs would also help reduce out-of-pocket spending on health, of course.

VSS Revenues and Expenditures—Recent Trends

In addition to expanding and deepening insurance coverage, Vietnam's health insurance program faces a further challenge: its financial sustainability. Since 2003, outlays have risen faster than revenues in both the compulsory and voluntary programs (figure 3.4). By 2005, outlays exceeded revenues in the voluntary program, and did so too in the compulsory program in 2006.

Figure 3.4: VSS's Changing Financial Fortunes, 2003–06

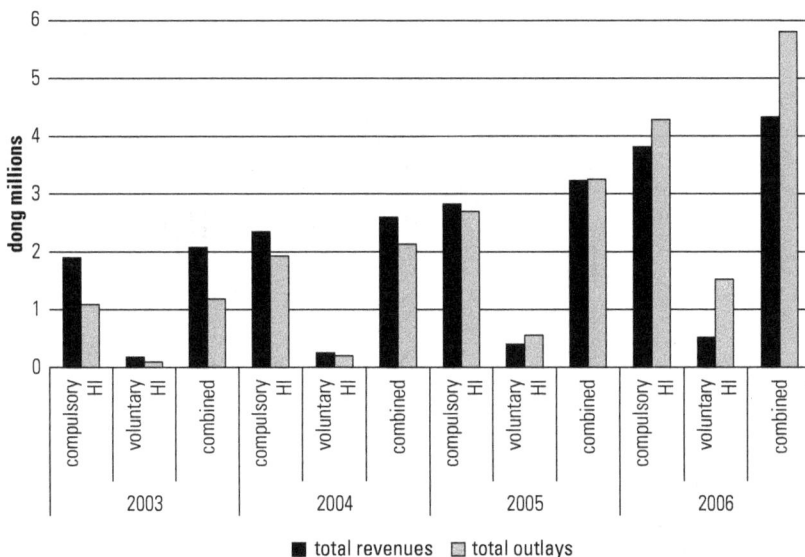

■ total revenues   ☐ total outlays

Source: Vietnam Social Security.

This change reflects two things: a shift in the mix of enrollees toward groups whose revenues are particularly low relative to the revenues they bring to the fund; and a tendency for outlays per enrollee to outpace revenues per enrollee. Formal sector workers accounted for one-quarter of all enrollees in 2005, brought in 57 percent of revenues, but accounted for only 32 percent of costs (figure 3.5). Pensioners, in contrast, accounted for only 8 percent of enrollees, but accounted for 20 percent of revenues and 29 percent of costs. The voluntary insured (mostly farmers) and Decision 139 beneficiaries are among the groups whose revenues fall short of the VSS outlays on their behalf. As is clear from figure 3.1, the recent growth of VSS enrollments has come primarily from these groups. This has contributed to the emergence of VSS's deficit. The more important factor, however, has been the rapid rise in

Figure 3.5: Costs and Revenues of Vietnam's Insurance Scheme, 2005

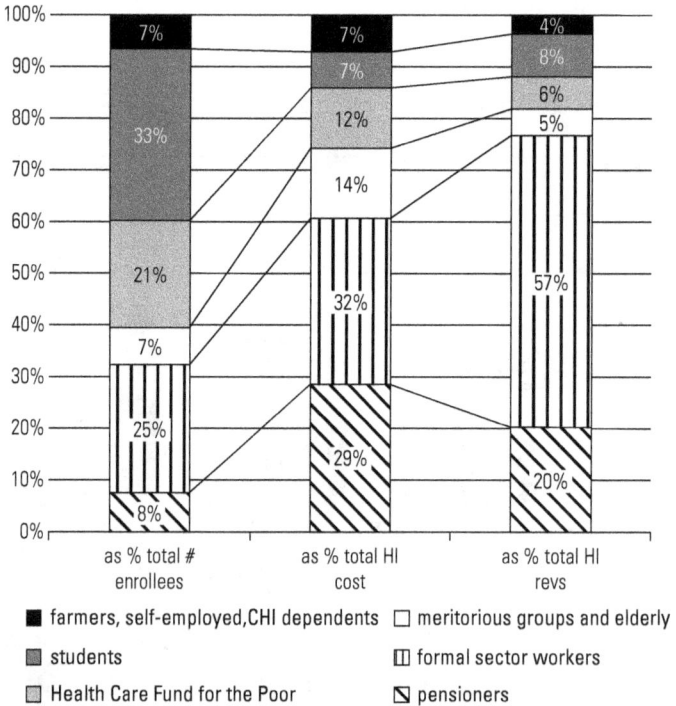

Source: Vietnam Social Security.

outlays per enrollee—an increase that has far exceeded the growth in revenues per enrollee (table 3.3). Revenue growth (per enrollee) has been driven largely by higher contributions from formal sector workers as wages have risen. Outlays per enrollee have increased especially quickly in the voluntary program. Increases in unit costs in the pensioner and student schemes have also contributed to VSS cost inflation.

Why have VSS outlays per enrollee risen so quickly? VSS has experienced increasing outlays per enrollee for both outpatient and inpatient care. These increases reflect both increased utilization rates and higher costs per case (figure 3.6).

Have VSS outlays per admission and outpatient visit increased faster than costs incurred by non-VSS patients? This is not easy to answer as VSS pays specific amounts (usually directly to providers) when it comes to care provided to VSS patients, while providers receive budgets from government and fees from patients to cover the costs of care provided to non-VSS patients. What can be done is to estimate the marginal cost of inpatient admissions and outpatient visits in Vietnam's hospitals using the hospital inventory dataset, and then compare the marginal costs and their changes with VSS outlays per case. Marginal costs for inpatient care in hospitals in general are higher

Table 3.3: VSS Revenues and Outlays per Person

	2003	2004	2005	2006
Pensioners	198.09	208.55	380.97	315.56
	254.60	324.81	479.07	717.06
Formal sector workers	253.83	262.73	321.93	352.90
	76.08	105.72	162.80	259.28
Meritorious group and elderly	110.87	100.66	101.22	121.50
	136.35	170.95	238.22	264.87
Health Care Fund for the Poor	30.70	40.85	42.37	48.94
	33.75	51.87	71.02	56.41
Students	35.44	36.10	35.28	45.00
	16.44	18.97	26.40	55.83
Others	90.53	74.14	78.62	110.87
		65.22	136.47	701.44
Total	119.91	120.51	160.07	165.80
	103.44	122.92	185.66	342.48

Source: Vietnam Social Security. The first line shows revenues, the second outlays.

Figure 3.6: Rising Unit Costs and Rising Utilization Rates as Causes of VSS's Financial Problems, 2004–06

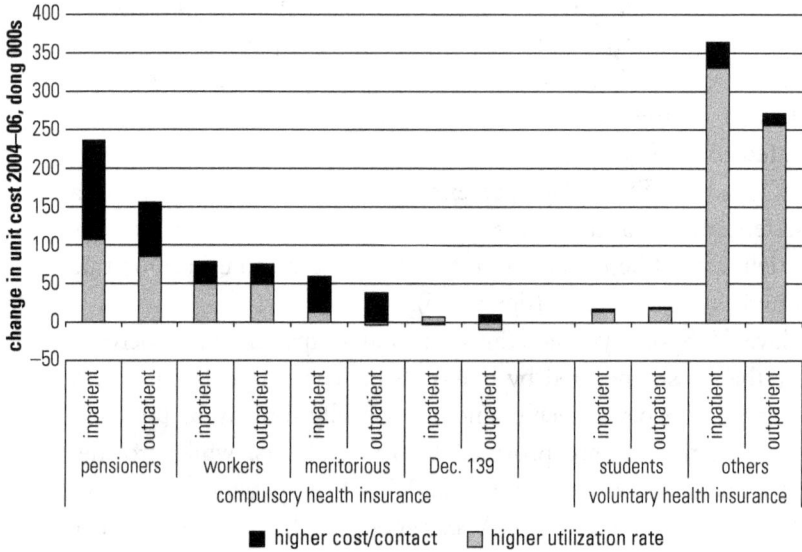

Source: Authors' calculations from VSS data.

than VSS reimbursements per inpatient admission (figure 3.7), confirming that VSS patients are subsidized. The figures also show, however, that VSS inpatient outlays per admission have increased faster than inpatient marginal costs among hospitals in general. As far as outpatient visits are concerned, VSS outlays per contact are lower than the marginal cost incurred by hospitals. However, VSS reimburses for outpatient visits at commune health centers as well as at hospitals, and in Vietnam, most outpatient visits occur outside a hospital.[11] In terms of trends, the figures show that VSS outlays per outpatient visit have increased more quickly than marginal costs for outpatient visits in hospitals generally. It could be that marginal costs for outpatient care have risen faster in CHCs than in hospitals, but it seems unlikely. In sum, VSS outlays per inpatient admission and outpatient visit do seem to have risen faster than (marginal) costs incurred by hospitals in treating the population at large.

Have utilization rates among VSS enrollees been increasing faster than among the population at large? The answer is "yes" as far as

Figure 3.7: Have VSS Inpatient and Outpatient Costs Risen Faster Than Those in the Health System as a Whole?

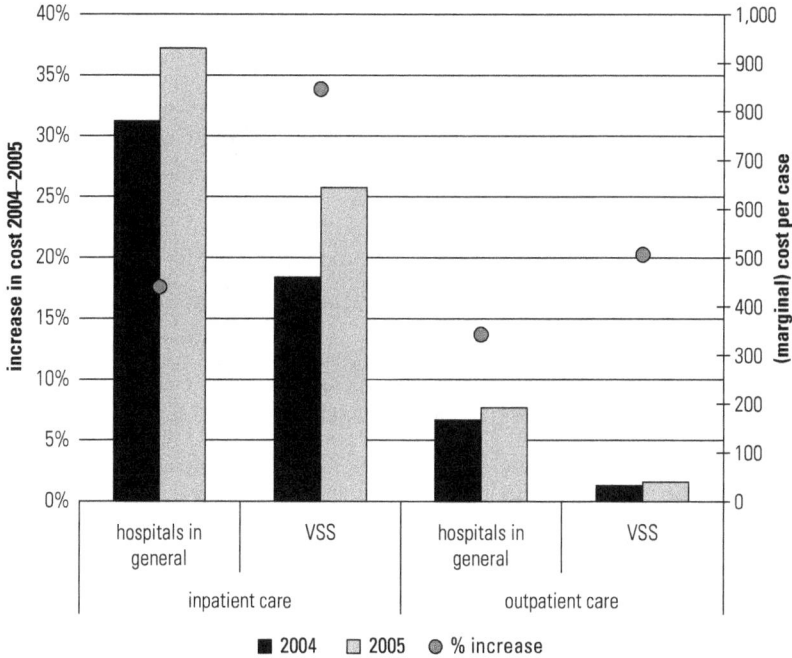

Source: Authors' calculations from VSS data and MOH hospital inventory. Marginal costs estimated using cost function proposed by Granneman et al., with same coefficients assumed for 2004 and 2005, but hospital-specific fixed effects allowed.

inpatient care is concerned (figure 3.8). Among the population as a whole, inpatient admissions increased on average by 5 percent per year between 2003 and 2006, while among VSS enrollees they increased by 11 percent per year. In contrast, VSS enrollees have recorded a smaller rate of growth of outpatient visits—8 percent compared to 19 percent.

Adverse Selection and Factors Affecting Coverage

For inpatient care, then, VSS has experienced growth rates of admissions and costs that exceed those among the population at large. For outpatient care, the utilization rate has grown more slowly among

Figure 3.8: Utilization Rates over Time for VSS Members and Vietnam's Population as a Whole

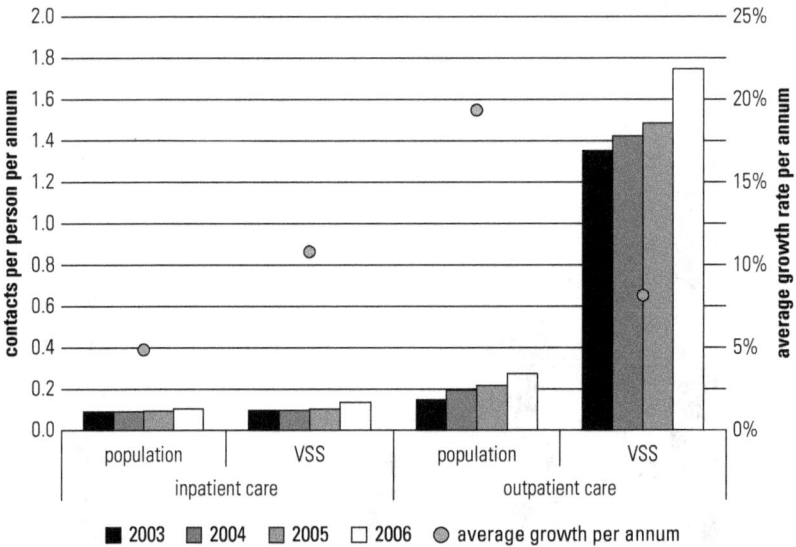

Source: Authors' calculations from VSS data and MOH Health Statistics Yearbook (various years). The population data reflect inpatient admissions and numbers of outpatients in all facilities including commune health centers.

VSS enrollees than among the population at large, but the cost has risen more quickly. Two explanations suggest themselves, both of which are likely to be at least partly true. Determining which is "truer" is impossible with existing data.

The first is that **adverse selection** is becoming more serious for VSS. According to this view, worse risks are increasingly likely to join the voluntary schemes, and local governments increasingly likely to enroll the worse risks among the under-six children and Decision 139 target population, issuing the healthy a health card instead. The latter is good from the point of view of targeting government resources on those most in need, but adverse selection worsens VSS's risk profile; if this is not taken into account when premiums and contributions are set, the result will be that VSS will inevitably run a deficit. Adverse selection can lead to the eventual collapse of a health insurance scheme, sometimes termed the health insurance "death spiral." Insurers soon enough realize that their enrollees are not average risks, and that their revenues are insufficient to cover their outlays. They raise their premiums and contributions to cover the deficit, which prompts disenrollment by the best risks, who find that at the higher premium, insurance is not worthwhile. The risk profile worsens, leaving the insurer with a deficit even after raising premiums. The process continues until the scheme collapses.

It seems to be the case that all of the schemes suffer from adverse selection. Whether or not the problem has gotten worse is impossible to say for sure with existing data. One sign that adverse selection is a problem comes from the 2006 VHLSS, which asks uninsured people why they are not covered. Their answers are revealing (figure 3.9). The most common response to the voluntary programs is that people consider themselves healthy enough not to need health insurance. But interestingly, this is also a common response among formal sector workers. We investigate below whether this hint of an adverse selection problem is borne out by more thorough analysis. Also interesting is the fact that good health is cited as a factor for noncoverage even among people who are entitled to coverage under Decision 139. Lack of affordability of insurance is also a common response, again intriguingly also among Decision 139 beneficiaries—indeed, among this group, this is the most common reason given for noncoverage. Not knowing where to obtain health insurance also emerges as important, again even among those entitled to cover under Decision 139. These results suggest an information problem, a deliberate policy on the part of the respondent's province to provide coverage through the health card scheme rather than through insurance, or a combination of the two.

Adverse selection emerges as a problem in more thorough analysis of the factors affecting coverage. This further analysis is also useful because it allows us to see the factors that affect which program people end up in and not just whether they are covered. This is helpful for an understanding of what factors constrain coverage. A statistical (multinomial logit) model was used to link the type of coverage an individual has (including no coverage as one of the categories) to a variety of possible factors that may influence the coverage the individual has. One key variable in exploring adverse selection is illness, the hypothesis being that the sicker are more likely to enroll or be enrolled. The 2006

Figure 3.9: Reasons Given for Noncoverage, 2006

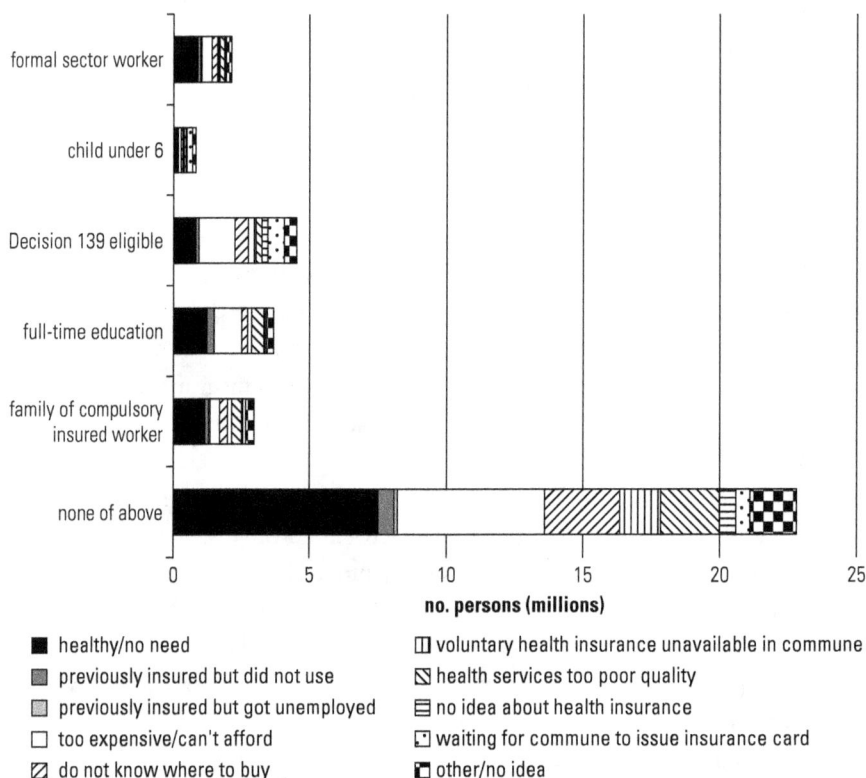

Legend:

- ■ healthy/no need
- ■ previously insured but did not use
- ▨ previously insured but got unemployed
- □ too expensive/can't afford
- ▨ do not know where to buy
- ⊞ voluntary health insurance unavailable in commune
- ▨ health services too poor quality
- ⊟ no idea about health insurance
- ▣ waiting for commune to issue insurance card
- ▪ other/no idea

Source: Authors' calculations from 2006 Vietnam Household and Living Standards Survey.

VHLSS—like the other living standards surveys in Vietnam—has limited information on illness. Illness occurring during the last 4 weeks or 12 months is recorded, but the existence of chronic illness and self-assessed health are not.[12] A separate analysis is undertaken for each target group. The results, which are shown in part in figure 3.10, reveal the following:

- Among **formal sector workers**, illness (either during the last four weeks or over the last year) does not significantly increase the probability of a worker being in the mandatory earnings-related contributory program rather than not being covered at all. (The latter outcome is the comparator throughout these

Figure 3.10: Effect of Illness on Probability of Coverage, 2006

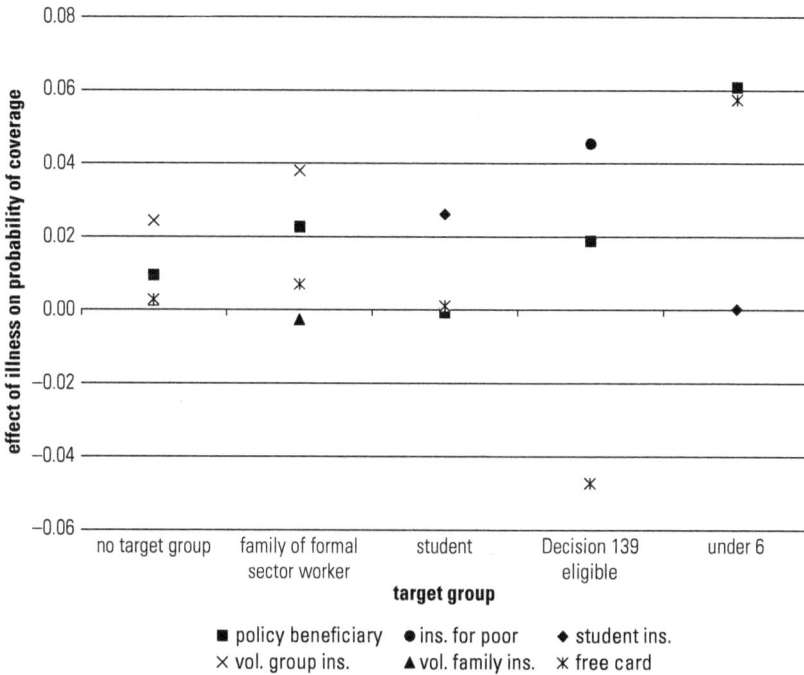

results.) Older people *are*, however, more likely to be enrolled in the contributory program, as are women. Both groups are likely to be above-average risks from an actuarial perspective, so this result does suggest some adverse selection. Those earning more and those who are more senior in their job are more likely to enroll, which from an actuarial perspective is probably good news. The collective sector, the private sector, and the foreign-invested sector are all less likely to enroll their workers. This is particularly true for the private sector. Workers living in the northeast and Central Highlands regions are more likely to be covered by the contributory scheme.

- In the case of **children ages 6 or less**, there is some evidence of adverse selection. Illness during the previous 12 months signifi-cantly increases the chances of a child ending up as a policy ben-eficiary or in receipt of a health card (figure 3.10). Older children are significantly less likely to be covered as a policy beneficiary or to get a health card, but are significantly more likely to be covered by the student program. This is consistent with provinces withdrawing coverage under the compulsory insurance program as under-six children begin attending school. Regional differences emerge as well. For example, under-six children living in the southeast are significantly less likely to be covered by the under-six program or the health card scheme. No clear income effects emerge among children under six.

• Adverse selection also seems to be an issue in how **Decision 139 beneficiaries** are treated. Illness significantly increases the chances of someone who is eligible for coverage under the program being covered as a policy beneficiary, and increases their chances of being enrolled in the Health Care Fund for the Poor program by an even larger degree (figure 3.10). In contrast, illness reduces (albeit not significantly) their chances of receiving a health certificate (rather than not being covered). This suggests that provinces are enrolling sick Decision 139 target individuals in the insurance program (hoping presumably to get the VSS program as a whole to help with the cost), but issuing health cards to the more healthy (perhaps hoping to make a "profit" on the Decision 139 subsidies from Hanoi). This behavior clearly undermines the principle of insurance. Interestingly, among Decision 139 target individuals, income reduces the likelihood of someone being included in the Health Care Fund for the Poor program, or being issued a health card. Living in the north of the country significantly increases the odds of a Decision 139 target individual receiving a health card, but does not significantly affect his or her chances of receiving health insurance. Thus, beneficiaries of Decision 139 living in the north are more likely to end up being given a health card than enrolled in the insurance program. Target individuals in the southeast and Mekong Delta regions, in contrast, are less likely to be covered by either program, other things being equal, with relative odds favoring coverage via a free health card in the Mekong and insurance in the southeast.

- Among **students,** the evidence is mixed on the issue of adverse selection. Illness over the last 12 months significantly raises the chances of a student being in the student scheme, compared to having no coverage (figure 3.10), while illness in the last 4 weeks has the opposite effect. Older students are significantly less likely to be covered under the student program, while students from better-off families are significantly *more* likely to be covered. Regional differences are also apparent: students in the southeast and Mekong Delta are, other things being equal, significantly less likely to be covered by the program.

- Among **families of formal sector workers**, there is some evidence of adverse selection into the voluntary program and the policy beneficiary scheme: illness over the last 12 months significantly raises the odds in both cases (figure 3.10). Better-off families are more likely to be covered in the voluntary scheme.

- There is strong evidence of adverse selection on long-term and recent illness into the voluntary program, and into the policy beneficiary scheme among the 30 million **people who fall into none of the target groups** (figure 3.10). Holding illness constant, income also significantly increases the odds of coverage in these programs, but significantly reduces the likelihood of someone in this group being issued a health card. Age increases the likelihood of coverage under all of the aforementioned schemes, but especially in the policy beneficiary scheme, presumably reflecting the fact that this group includes retired government and party officials, who have not been separately identified in the analysis, but who are a target group in their own right (along with other "persons of merit"). There are interesting regional differences as well: for example, living in the Mekong Delta increases the odds that someone will be in a voluntary scheme and reduces the odds they will covered as a policy beneficiary or issued a health card.

Finally, yet more evidence of adverse selection emerges if we analyze factors affecting uninsured people's responses to the hypothetical question "If health insurance were available at D 80,000 per annum, would you enroll?" Among people who fall into none of the target groups, illness in the last four weeks and last year significantly increase the chances of them saying "yes." Illness during the last four weeks also significantly raises the probability of a yes answer among family members of a formal sector worker and people who are entitled to be covered through Decision 139, but are not. Among these three groups, the elderly are more likely to say "yes," as are women. Among all groups except family members of formal sector workers and parents answering on behalf of under-six children, a higher income is associated with a higher probability of answering yes to the hypothetical insurance question. Thus, as in actual enrollment decisions, the responses to the hypothetical question point to adverse selection and inequity associated with income as being major challenges with a voluntary approach to insurance.

There seems, then, to be fairly clear evidence that health insurance does indeed suffer from adverse selection. It is not altogether surprising that the voluntary programs are plagued by it. Nor, perhaps, is it particularly surprising that there is also some adverse selection (in respect to age and gender) in the formal sector workers' program. What is perhaps more surprising is the fact that adverse selection operates in the under-six and Decision 139 programs as well. The results imply that young children who are sick are more likely to be enrolled in the under-six program, a laudable outcome from the point of view of targeting, but a financial disaster for VSS and Bao Viet, which rely on both good and bad risks enrolling to break even, given that premiums and contributions are based on average risks, not bad risks. Also worrying for the same reason is the finding that sick Decision 139 beneficiaries are significantly more likely to be steered toward VSS, while the good risks are issued health cards. Again, this undermines the principle of insurance—VSS requires both groups if it is to remain solvent.

While these results point to adverse selection existing in 2006, they do not tell us whether the problem has become worse in recent years. However, the deterioration in VSS's finances, and the reasons for it, are consistent with worsening adverse selection being the culprit. But there is a second hypothesis that could also explain the trend.

Moral Hazard and the Impacts of Health Insurance

This second hypothesis is that **moral hazard** has worsened. The term "moral hazard" refers to the idea that once people are insured, they pay a price for health care that is below cost, and will consume care beyond the point where the marginal benefit of care is equal to its marginal cost. Not all of the increase in health care utilization associated with insurance, however, is moral hazard (Nyman 1999). Part of the increase reflects the transfer of resources through risk pooling from those who have been lucky enough not to fall sick to those who have had the misfortune to do so. This part of the increase in utilization is not a welfare loss; it is, in fact, an important part of the welfare gain from insurance. What moral hazard refers to is the increase in utilization on top of this resource transfer-induced increase in utilization that reflects the fact that the price of health care has fallen relative to the prices of other goods and services, and this causes the insured to substitute toward health care and away from other goods and services. This substitution is inefficient for society as a whole and represents a welfare loss, because the price of health care to society is the same as it was before insurance.

Separating the increase in utilization associated with insurance into the part due to moral hazard and the part due to the transfer of resources from the healthy to the sick is not straightforward, and few studies seek to do it, with many erroneously labeling the whole increase in utilization associated with insurance as "moral hazard." One author (Nyman 1999), using U.S. estimates, suggests that the moral hazard effect might be as little as one-third of the insurance effect. As mentioned earlier, studies from Vietnam suggest that insurance has led to increases in utilization, especially hospital care. Some of this likely reflects moral hazard. This likelihood is increased by the way providers are paid. It is widely accepted in Vietnam that FFS encourages providers to deliver health care that may not be medically necessary, or at least may not produce large enough health benefits to justify the extra expense. When patients pick up part of the bill via copayments, even they may feel the health benefits of the extra care are too small to warrant the extra out-of-pocket spending. The patient's problem, of course, is that he rarely knows enough about medicine to make this judgment. With providers facing such strong incentives to deliver extra care, the likelihood is that any demand-side moral hazard is reinforced by supply-side moral hazard.

Is moral hazard getting worse? There is no firm evidence on the subject. It is, however, widely believed that moral hazard became a bigger problem when the 20 percent coinsurance rate was scrapped in mid-2005. There is probably some truth to this, but outlays per enrollee increased by a high percentage in the year before the change as well: in 2004, outlays per enrollee increased by 25 percent, compared to 38 percent in 2005.

What can safely be said is that insurance in Vietnam has probably encouraged *some* overuse of services, but exactly how much is not known. Nor is it known—and probably never will be—how much was caused by the patient being too keen to seek care in the first place and how much was due to the provider being too keen to deliver care, spurred on by the promise of higher revenues. Curbing overuse of care caused by insurance is one challenge facing VSS in its efforts to cut costs. But it is not the only one: reducing adverse selection is also important.

CHAPTER 4

Reforming Health Insurance

Vietnam's health insurance system faces three major challenges: expanding coverage to a larger section of the population; deepening coverage so that patients pay a smaller fraction of the cost out of pocket; and containing costs. Figure 4.1 shows the challenge in terms of expanding the fraction of the population covered, while figure 4.2 shows the challenge in terms of shifting the financing mix away from out-of-pocket payments. Comparing the two charts reveals an important point that needs to be kept in mind: the current mandatory and voluntary schemes together cover 40 percent of the population, but account for only 13 percent of total health expenditure. Figure 4.3 shows the information in figure 4.2 in terms of financial flows among the various "actors" in the health system.

The first step is to expand coverage. There is no agreement internationally on how best to do this. The chapter explores three options: expanding coverage within the existing policy framework; moving toward a mandatory contributions-based scheme for everyone except the poor, who would continue to be financed at taxpayers' expense as at present; and a universal program with formal sector workers contributing according to their earnings and everyone else's coverage being financed at taxpayers' expense. The fiscal implications of the third option are explored in some depth; they turn out not to be as daunting as one might expect, due in part to Vietnam's small fiscal deficit and in part to the fact that the government is credibly committed to expanding its revenues, in part through a broadening of its revenue base.

Figure 4.1: Insurance Coverage by Scheme

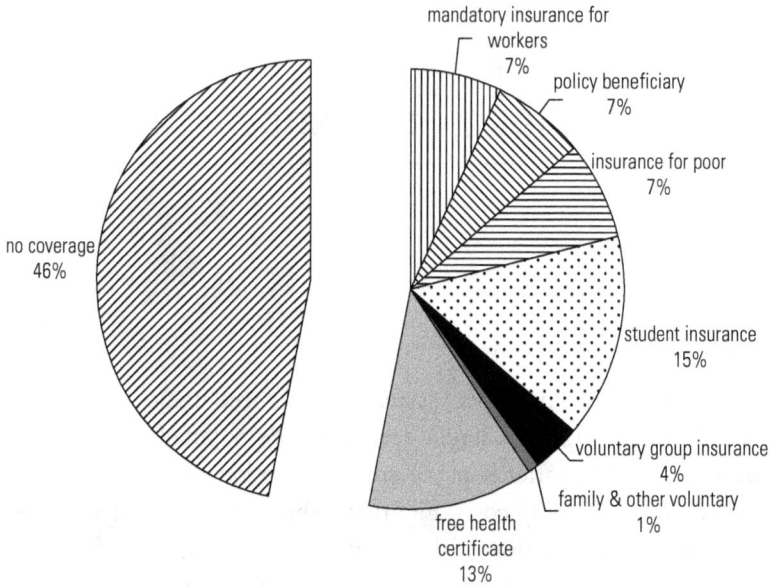

mandatory insurance for
workers
7%

policy beneficiary
7%

insurance for poor
7%

student insurance
15%

voluntary group insurance
4%

family & other voluntary
1%

free health
certificate
13%

no coverage
46%

Figure 4.2: Current Financing Mix in Vietnam

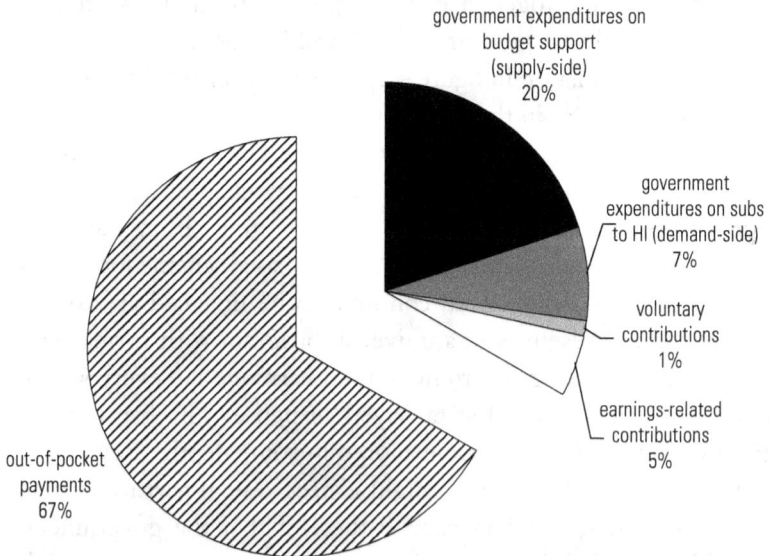

government expenditures on
budget support
(supply-side)
20%

government
expenditures on subs
to HI (demand-side)
7%

voluntary
contributions
1%

earnings-related
contributions
5%

out-of-pocket
payments
67%

Notes: Estimates based on WHO NHA, VSS statistics, and VHLSS 2006 Household Survey data. Taxes for HI are to cover the VSS deficit and enrollees in the compulsory program financed out of the state budget.

Figure 4.3: Financial Flows in Current System

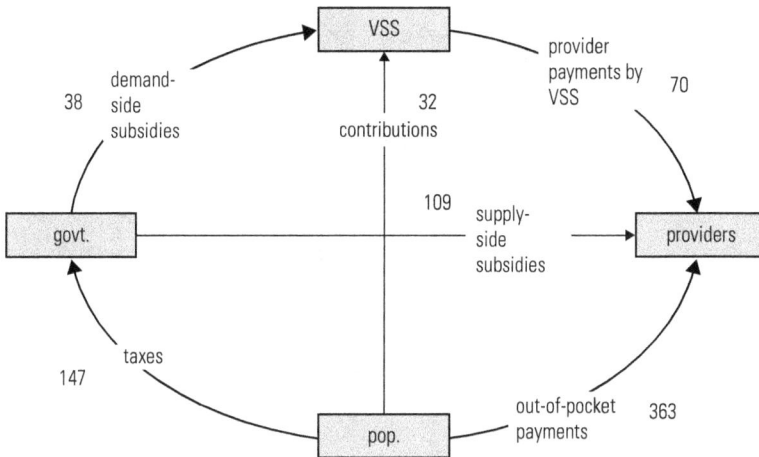

All of these approaches, even in the best scenario, will simply expand coverage to 100 percent of the population. Given the current way insurance works in Vietnam, they will all leave out-of-pocket payments as the major source of health finance. So, the second step will be to *deepen* coverage. Deepening coverage requires that someone other than the patient picks up a larger fraction of the provider's costs. This could involve higher supply-side subsidies. Or it could involve an upward revision of the fee schedule for VSS (and uninsured patients). The relative merits of each approach depend on the fraction of the population covered by the insurance scheme. The more successful the government is in expanding coverage, the stronger the case for uprating the fee schedule and making VSS the dominant payer in the health system. This would necessitate an increase in VSS revenues, of course, which would require increased contributions and demand-side subsidies, with larger implied increases in government spending in the scenarios where coverage is expanded through an expansion of tax-financed coverage. If the fee schedule is uprated and VSS contributions are increased to accommodate the extra VSS outlays, care would need to be taken to ensure that providers reduce their charges to patients, rather than try to "capture" the extra fee income and hold on to their out-of-pocket payment income.

In tandem with expanding and deepening coverage, there need to be efforts to put downward pressure on VSS's costs, especially its outlays for health services. On cost containment strategies for insurers, there is also a lack of consensus internationally. There is disagreement, for example, on the effectiveness of copayments as a tool for tackling moral hazard, and on what ought to be included in a benefit package. In contrast, there is considerable agreement that certain ways of paying providers do better than others at promoting cost consciousness. There is also an emerging consensus that clinical guidelines may play an important role in containing costs. These strategies all have implications for the way health care providers operate, and are both health financing issues and service delivery issues. Some aspects are therefore picked up again in the service delivery chapter.

Expanding Coverage

Vietnam has essentially three options for expanding coverage beyond the current 40 percent of the population.

(i) The first is to expand coverage within the existing policy framework, by ensuring that the target groups are indeed covered (whether at their own expense or at the taxpayers'), and by persuading those not in the target groups to enroll voluntarily.

(ii) The second would be to make health insurance mandatory for everyone, requiring that everyone not covered by Decision 139 sign up and contribute to the health insurance scheme.

(iii) The third option would be to use general revenues (tax and nontax revenues, and grants) to cover all individuals not in the compulsory scheme, not just the Decision 139 and other policy beneficiaries.

Each is considered in turn.

Expanding Coverage within the Existing Policy Framework

Expanding coverage within the existing policy framework beyond the groups already covered is likely to prove harder than it has been covering those already included. Those already in the scheme are easily identified, and enforcement in some groups is quite straightforward. The formal sector workers in the government sector are not only easily identified, but their enrollment is easily enforced. Other groups have been less easy to identify and enforcement has been less straightforward. There has been considerable success identifying the poor and other Decision 139 beneficiaries, but less success getting provinces to enroll the beneficiaries in VSS, rather than covering them through the direct reimbursement modality. Enrollment among formal sector workers who are not government employees has largely been hampered by lax enforcement, though some who are not enrolled claim they do not know how to do so. In a sense, the low-hanging fruit has already been picked.

There are, however, things that could be done to expand coverage within the existing policy framework. Enforcing enrollment among formal sector workers—especially the private sector—is one such step. An estimated 2.2 million formal sector workers currently lack coverage of any type. As was seen in figure 3.3, rates of nonenrollment are higher in some sectors than others. Compliance could be increased by fining noncomplying organizations, perhaps with fines that increase in size month by month over, say, a two-year period. Random checks on organizations, targeting especially those with low rates of coverage according to figure 3.3, would likely be a necessary part of this strategy. Over the longer term, VSS would need to build up a comprehensive database; this could usefully be linked to the government's business taxation database, since businesses are required to pay various taxes, such as VAT, and in some cases corporate income tax as well.

One challenge in increasing compliance in the formal sector is the link to the compulsory pension program: The target groups are much the same and enrollment numbers seem to be similar.[13] This is an advantage in one sense, but also a disadvantage. It is an advantage in that efforts to enforce enrollment can be combined. It is a disadvantage in that the incentive to enroll in health insurance is linked to the incentive to enroll in the pensions program—workers cannot choose to enroll in one but not the other. This would be less of a problem if the contributory program were an attractive deal financially for private sector workers. But it is not. Simulations in the 2008 Vietnam Development Report indicate that a private sector worker with less than 20 years left before retirement would do better to save for himself (World Bank 2007). And for those with more than 20 years left until retirement, it makes sense to contribute only for 30 years in total. This suggests that reforming pensions to make them more attractive financially to private sector workers will be vital to encouraging enrollment in the mandatory health insurance program among private sector workers.

Bringing in the 4.7 million people who are supposed to be covered under Decision 139 but who do not have any coverage is also important. It is also highly desirable—from the point of view of ensuring VSS's financial solvency—that those under-six children and Decision 139 beneficiaries who currently have a free health card rather than a health insurance card also be brought into the health insurance scheme. Given the finding above that geography influences people's probability of being in the scheme, it would make sense to focus on bringing recalcitrant provincial governments into line with the government policy that all under-six children and Decision 139 beneficiaries be covered by the health insurance scheme.

Expanding enrollment in the voluntary programs will be much harder, since nonenrollment tends to be a conscious decision by most of the currently nonenrolled, who judge the cost to be too high compared to the benefits involved given their state of health. Changing the rules concerning formal sector workers so that the scheme covers workers and their dependents—a recently discussed idea—is a possibility worth considering. It could bring in a further 3.1 million people. This step would entail an increase in the contribution rate from the current 3 percent to something considerably higher, given that of the various household members the worker is probably the least costly for VSS to cover. The risk with this approach is that it will make formal sector workers and their employers even less keen to enroll in the insurance program.

Subsidizing voluntary enrollment for the near-poor—a recent policy measure—will help, though exactly how much remains to be seen, not least of all because it is unclear how the near-poor are to be identified. Raising the subsidy to 70 percent would clearly have a bigger impact than the current 30 percent subsidy. Removing the requirement that households enroll as a whole and that community groups achieve a 20 percent membership threshold before anyone can join would also help raise enrollment revenues, but again it is unclear by how much.

Mandatory Contributory Insurance

While all these measures would help raise enrollment levels, the probability is that, even with such measures, the government will hit a coverage ceiling, and this will probably be some way below 100 percent. Exactly how far below is very hard to say, since it would depend on the measures adopted and their enforcement. Alternatives are therefore worth considering.

One would be mandatory insurance. Insurance is already mandatory for formal sector workers (although enrollment is not fully enforced), and the poor and other Decision 139 beneficiaries are covered at the government's expense (or are supposed to be). The idea would be to step up efforts to cover these and other existing target groups (such as the under-six and students), and require that everyone who is not a member of a target group (27 million people) enroll with VSS at their own expense.

Several measures could be adopted to improve the prospects of this approach. As above, formal sector workers could be required to enroll their family members. If successful, this would bring in 3 million people. To increase the chances of the other 24 million people enrolling, there could be some linking of contributions to income. The near-poor could have their contributions subsidized, though as mentioned above, this would require that they be capable of being identified. Linking contributions to household income—as happens among the informal sectors of several OECD countries including Korea, as well as non-OECD advanced economies like Taiwan—is likely to be unrealistic at Vietnam's current state of development because documenting incomes and preventing evasion and underreporting are very difficult in a society where the informal economy is the dominant economy for a large section of the population. This is precisely what has plagued Vietnam's personal income tax (PIT) system: Currently in Vietnam, only 0.2 percent of households pay PIT, all in the richest quintile.

There are a couple of things that could be done, however. One would be to levy higher contributions in richer areas—as happens at present. This process could be made even more sophisticated through the use of poverty maps—linking contributions to the estimated average income of the area in which the person lives. There may also be some scope for the use of proxy means testing, a method that is widely used in social programs around the world to identify households that are eligible for subsidized food, schooling, and health services. Colombia's *Sistema de Identificación de Potenciales Beneficiarios de Programas Sociales* (SISBEN) or system of identifying potential beneficiaries of social programs index is an example of such a scheme, the use of which has made the subsidized health insurance regime of that country one of the best targeted of all public subsidies (Escobar 2005).[14]

Sanctions would need to be imposed to ensure that people complied with the mandatory insurance requirement. There may be some scope for fining employers who contract with self-employed professionals, as happens in Colombia, but getting employers to enroll their own staffs is proving quite a challenge in itself in Vietnam. There may be scope for use of mass movement organizations such as the Vietnam Farmers' Union, the Vietnam Women's Union and the Ho Chi Minh Communist Youth Union in Vietnam to play a part in the enforcement process, or for these mass movement organizations to facilitate the enrollment process by being a bridge between enrollees and VSS.

Mandatory insurance also has its problems. The collection of contributions and enforcing of enrollment would be costly. VSS already incurs 8 percent of its outlays in the voluntary scheme on paying agents to enroll people and issue cards. Linking contributions to income is not easy to set up, and the simplest options are likely to be the ones that are likely to command the least support, being perceived as unrefined and unfair.

Universal Health Insurance

The option of mandatory health insurance is worth considering, but it is not without its problems, and it is not at all clear that it would be successful in taking Vietnam to universal coverage, or even close to it. A more radical option would to be to move toward a universal health insurance scheme, run by VSS and financed through a mix of contributions (paid by formal sector workers) and the government budget (for others). This is the direction that Thailand recently opted for in its 30-baht scheme (Pannarunothai et al. 2004; Towse et al. 2004). One obvious question is whether such an approach would be fiscally viable in Vietnam (see table 4.1).

Expanding VSS coverage to the entire population would raise VSS outlays, and these extra outlays would have to be financed somehow. We assume that those who are currently uninsured have the same inpatient admission and outpatient visit rates as those who are currently insured, and that VSS will spend the same amount per contact for the newly insured as it spends on those currently insured. Under these assumptions, expanding coverage to 100 percent of the population would raise VSS outlays from D 5,804 billion to D 12,102 billion, or from D 70,000 per capita to D 147,000 per capita, an increase of D 77,000 per capita.[15] The data refer to 2006 values.

The increase in government spending is likely to be larger than this, because if VSS coverage is extended to include those currently uncovered, there may be a need to make changes to the contributions of those already enrolled. Most obviously, it would be hard to get people to continue to enroll voluntarily with VSS if their neighbors and friends are being covered by the taxpayer. If voluntary enrollment were eliminated, an extra D 6,000 per capita (D 0.5 trillion) worth of government spending would be incurred on top of the D 77,000 per capita above.

There may also be pressure in such a system to reduce contributions by formal sector workers in the longer term. The reason is that people have a reduced incentive to move into formal employment if by staying self-employed they can keep the same health insurance coverage but avoid insurance contributions. One way to reduce this risk would be to have a lower contribution rate for people joining the formal sector (i.e. in their first formal sector job)— perhaps close to zero in the first year of employment and rising to the regular rate gradually over, say, a five-year period. In the longer term, as the tax base broadens, the government might want to reconsider whether it makes sense to keep a contributory scheme

Table 4.1: Simulating the Costs of Universal Insurance

Population 82.48 million

GDP per capita dong 11,806,000

	CURRENT (2006)	100% COVERAGE, ADDITIONAL COVERAGE FINANCED BY GOVT. SPENDING, CURRENT DEPTH OF COVERAGE	100% COVERAGE, ADDITIONAL COVERAGE FINANCED BY GOVT. SPENDING, DOUBLE VSS REVENUES
VND billions			
Government expenditures on budget support (supply-side)	9,000	9,000	9,000
Government expenditures on subs to HI (demand-side)	3,155	9,973	19,946
Voluntary contributions	520	0	0
Earnings-related contributions	2,129	2,129	4,259
Out-of-pocket payments	29,901	26,664	14,561
Total	*44,706*	*47,766*	*47,766*
OOP share (%)	67%	56%	30%
VSS outlays	5,804	12,102	24,205
Government expenditures on health care	12,155	18,973	28,946
General government expenditures on health care	14,804	21,102	33,205
Overall government expenditures incl. VSS contributions	267,600	273,898	286,000
Extra general government expenditures compared to current		6,298	18,400
VND 000's per capita			
Government expenditures on budget support (supply-side)	109	109	109
Government expenditures on subs to HI (demand-side)	38	121	242
Voluntary contributions	6	0	0
Earnings-related contributions	26	26	52
Out-of-pocket payments	363	323	177
Total	*542*	*579*	*579*
VSS outlays	70	147	293
Government expenditures on health care	147	230	351
General government expenditures on health care	179	256	403
Overall government expenditures incl. VSS contributions	3,244	3,321	3,468
As % GDP			
General government expenditures on health care	1.5%	2.2%	3.4%
Private expenditures on health care	3.1%	2.7%	1.5%
Overall government expenditures incl. VSS contributions	27.5%	28.1%	29.4%
Fiscal deficit (current, and for scenario if extra spending financed through borrowing)	−3.9	−4.4	−5.7
Government revenues (current, and for scenario if extra spending financed through higher revenues)	27.1	27.8	29.0

alongside the noncontributory regime, and move instead to a non-contributory regime for everyone, gaining the benefits of a broad financing base.

On the assumption that general revenues would be used to finance coverage of all those not currently enrolled with VSS and all those voluntarily enrolled with VSS, but contributions remain at their existing level for formal sector workers, general government spending on health (i.e. inclusive of VSS contributions) would rise by a total of D 76,000 per capita, or D 6.3 trillion in aggregate. These changes would raise general government expenditure on health as a share of GDP from 1.5 percent to 2.2 percent—still below its "expected" share on the basis of international experience (see figure 1.4).

How could this extra government spending be financed? If this extra spending were financed entirely through additional borrowing, Vietnam's fiscal deficit would increase from 3.8 percent of GDP to 4.4 percent of GDP. This is not a major increase. However, alternatives are worth exploring. In fact, there are good reasons to think the extra spending could be financed through higher government revenues rather than extra borrowing. The first is that the population gains financially from insurance coverage expansion and ought to be willing to pay extra taxes as a quid pro quo. Part of the increased spending (D 6,000 per capita, or D 0.5 trillion in aggregate) is necessitated by a reduction in VSS contributions. Households could reasonably be asked to pay extra taxes in lieu of these contributions.

There is another respect in which households benefit financially from expanded insurance coverage—the newly insured are likely to pay less out of pocket for their health care than before. Using plausible assumptions, total out-of-pocket spending on health care would fall from D 29,901 billion (67 percent of total health expenditure) to D 26,664 billion (56 percent of total expenditure), a reduction of D 3.2 trillion, equivalent to an 11 percent fall. The relatively small reduction reflects two factors: the fact that coverage is fairly shallow so that on average insurance reduces out-of-pocket spending by only 18 percent; and the fact that 40 percent of the population already has insurance.[16] Asking households—as a whole—to pay extra taxes in exchange for the D 3.2 trillion reduction in out-of-pocket spending seems reasonable. The remaining D 2.7 trillion of the increase in government spending reflects the cost of providing extra health care that is not currently being delivered.

The fact that the case for raising an extra VND 6.7 trillion worth of government revenues for health is fairly reasonable does not mean that it is easy to raise them. However, as mentioned in chapter 1, the government is committed to looking for ways to expand revenues through a broadening of its revenue base. The Vietnam Development Report 2008: Social Protection (World Bank 2007) discussed a couple of tax reforms in depth, though other options are worth exploring, too. One of the two reforms is the scaling up of Vietnam's personal income tax system. Currently, PIT raises only around D 6 trillion. However, under a new regime that goes into effect in 2009, Vietnam's PIT is expected to raise nearly D 20 trillion. The other reform option is the introduction of a full-fledged property tax. Vietnam does have taxes and fees on land and property, but they raise only D 6 trillion to 7 trillion, equivalent to just 2.6 percent of government revenues. In contrast, in China property taxes account for 7.7 percent of general revenues, while in Australia, Canada, the United Kingdom, and the United States, they account for 9 percent to 14 percent (Ahmad 2008). A full-fledged property tax could raise significant revenues, and would have the twin merits of being strongly progressive and of causing relatively few distortions in economic behavior (taxes on wage income, for example, as already noted, discourage formal sector employment) (World Bank 2007).

Not mentioned in the Vietnam Development Report 2008: Social Protection, perhaps for reasons that will become clear, is another possible option, namely raising taxes on cigarettes. Like China (Hussain and Stern 2008), Vietnam combines a high incidence of male smoking (51 percent of adult males in Vietnam smoke) with a low tax rate (36 percent).[17] For example, India's cigarette tax rate is 75 percent, the Philippines' is 63 percent, and Thailand's is 62 percent. Only 7 of the 60 countries with published cigarette tax rates have a lower rate than Vietnam. Currently, cigarette taxes raise only around D 1.1 trillion and account for less than 1 percent of total government revenues (Van Kinh et al. 2006). One possibility would be to raise the current rates to a uniform rate of 65 percent. If this were done, however, the effect on tax revenues would be relatively modest, amounting to an extra D 1.2 trillion, an increase of just 11 percent (Van Kinh et al. 2006). The relatively small impact reflects the high price elasticity of demand for cigarettes in Vietnam, with people switching in response to price increases to other (largely untaxed) forms of tobacco, including chewing tobacco (Ramanan Laxminarayan 2004). Raising cigarette taxes would therefore not do much to help raise extra revenues for government health spending.

Deepening Coverage to Further Reduce Out-of-Pocket Payments

All of the measures outlined above are geared to expanding coverage to a larger fraction of the population. They do not deepen coverage, however. With the current coverage arrangements, health insurance reduces a person's expected out-of-pocket payments by about 18 percent, with larger percentage reductions for outpatient and inpatient expenditures (30 percent to 35 percent) and smaller reductions on drug and medical equipment expenditures. Even under the universal coverage scenario above, out-of-pocket payments would remain the dominant source of health care financing in Vietnam, accounting for 56 percent of total health spending. The second element to a successful reform of health insurance must therefore be to *deepen* coverage.

Why do the insured pay anything for health care? In part, the spending is on drugs bought from drug vendors, and on medical equipment. Some spending is on privately provided care as well. But out-of-pocket payments are also paid to public facilities. Sometimes they are formal copayments. But sometimes they are simply payments to providers to make up the shortfall between the cost of the service and the revenues the provider gets from VSS and the Health Ministry in the form of budget support. Payments by VSS are for both drugs and fees, the latter being determined by a government-set fee schedule. This schedule was established in 1995, and only the items added since then have prices that reflect current costs, though even these are below the full cost because of supply-side subsidies.

There are two ways, then, that the government could reduce the amount that the insured pay out of pocket. One would be to increase supply-side subsidies. The other would be to revise the fee schedule upward so that VSS picks up a larger fraction of the cost of care. The attraction of these two options depends on how successful the government is at expanding coverage, because currently the same fees apply to uninsured patients (who pay the fee out of pocket) as to insured patients (whose fees are paid by VSS). If a large fraction of the population is left uninsured, raising fees is not an attractive option; instead, the government would want to introduce more generous supply-side subsidies, since this would help reduce out-of-pocket payments for both insured and uninsured patients.

If, by contrast, most, if not all, of the population is covered, increasing fees *would* be an option. VSS would, of course, need more revenues if it is to cover the higher fees. This would mean raising contributions and raising demand-side subsidies to cover those who are enrolled at the taxpayers' expense. Of course, if contributions are increased and enrollment is not mandatory, or is mandatory for a part or all of the population, but is only weakly enforced, enrollment may be adversely affected—people who are already disinclined to enroll may be even more disinclined to enroll if contributions increase. The hope is that the higher contributions will result in improved financial protection through lower out-of-pocket payments, so that people will value the insurance coverage more.

What would happen to out-of-pocket payments if fees were raised and VSS contributions were raised accordingly? For out-of-pocket payments to fall, we would need to be confident that providers would reduce the payments they collect from insured patients. This might not actually happen. Providers are more likely to try to limit the drop in revenues from out-of-pocket payments by patients and take the opportunity to increase their incomes by enjoying *both* the higher fee income from VSS *and* continued out-of-pocket payment income from patients. That this might happen is suggested by evidence from the Philippines, where private hospitals have been very successful in topping up their payments from the insurer with out-of-pocket payment income from insured patients (Gertler and Solon 2000). They have been so successful, in fact, that the out-of-pocket payment income they earn from an insured patient is as large as the out-of-pocket payment income they earn from an uninsured patient.

In Vietnam, hospitals might be less successful, because of price regulation, which is absent in the Philippines (the success of hospitals there in charging insured patients so much is that hospitals can charge patients whatever they like and are able to charge insured patients more than uninsured patients for the same services). Nonetheless, it is worth being open to the possibility. Any upward revision of the fee schedule would need to be accompanied by steps to ensure that the out-of-pocket spending by insured patients is indeed falling as intended. VSS could have a role there, being charged with monitoring not just what it pays providers, but what its members pay out of pocket. This would mean that either patients or providers would need to supply VSS with information on out-of-pocket payments as part of the billing process.

Raising VSS contributions in the hope of deepening coverage would have public expenditure implications, of course. For example, in the third option above, if as well as expanding coverage to the currently uninsured at the taxpayers' expense, the government were to also double VSS revenues (a doubling of contributions from formal sector workers and a doubling of demand-side subsidies to cover others), government spending would increase by D 18.4 trillion rather than by D 6.3 trillion (the rise if coverage were expanded but not deepened). General government spending on health would reach 3.4 percent of GDP, a little above the "expected" fraction—see figure 1.5). If financed through borrowing, this would take the fiscal deficit from 3.9 percent of GDP to 5.7 percent, an appreciable worsening. If financed through higher government revenues, the share of GDP absorbed by taxes, fees, and grants would increase to 29 percent (currently it is 27 percent). This doubling of VSS outlays would leave out-of-pocket payments accounting for *at least* 30 percent of total health spending. This figure assumes that providers reduce their out-of-pocket payment income by one dong for every extra dong of revenue they get from VSS. This is an unrealistic assumption for the reasons given above, so out-of-pocket payments would account for well over 30 percent of total health spending even with universal coverage and a doubling of VSS revenues per member.

Reforms to Contain Health Insurance Program Costs

The final element of a successful health insurance reform would be the introduction of measures that exert downward pressure on the costs incurred by VSS—both its own administrative costs, but, more importantly, its outlays on health care.

A shift to a mandatory health insurance system would likely raise VSS's administrative costs, while a move to a universal scheme funded largely through general revenues would likely reduce them. Measures that reduce adverse selection will help ensure that VSS does not get left with the bad risks; the risk then is that VSS might be forced to raise contributions, thereby precipitating a death spiral, or it might forever need to find funds to cover its deficit. The risk of adverse selection is linked to the issue of coverage expansion. If a universal scheme were introduced, adverse selection would be eliminated automatically. If a mandatory scheme were introduced, adverse selection would be reduced, though probably not eliminated in the short run because there would likely be some who would not comply with the compulsory enrollment requirement. The proposals above for expanding coverage within the existing policy framework would help reduce adverse selection if they were successfully introduced as a package, but adverse selection would remain an issue.

Aside from reducing its administrative costs and improving its risk profile, VSS could also potentially lower its costs by reducing its outlays to providers. This could be achieved by putting downward pressure on the number of inpatient admissions and outpatient visits, or through a reduction in the cost per admission and cost per visit, or both. Of course, one would not want VSS to reduce these as far as possible. Hence, some guidance is required, as well as some oversight of VSS in its expenditure control efforts.

VSS ought, at least in principle, to be encouraged to reduce the degree of moral hazard, that is, patients overusing services as a result of facing a price at the point of use that is lower than the cost of care.

Copayments would be an obvious mechanism to address this. However, establishing the extent of moral hazard is not straightforward, and there is no consensus on how much moral hazard there is in Vietnam. Furthermore, because patients are poor judges of whether they need care and what type of care they need (that is precisely the reason they seek the advice of a medical provider in the first place), the likelihood is that copayments will be a poor instrument to tackle moral hazard, and that one might end up curbing utilization too far, especially among the poor. This is not to say that copayments should not have a role, rather that they should be used sparingly. And if they are reintroduced on care costing less than D 7 million (the current threshold), it would be desirable to exempt those covered by Decision 139.

Another way to reduce the volume of utilization would be to restrict the interventions covered by insurance, by having a benefit package that excludes more interventions than are currently excluded. One might introduce a voluntary supplementary insurance scheme to cover the interventions not covered by the basic VSS program. There are some risks to this approach, most obviously that by being voluntary, it is likely to be subject to adverse selection. Furthermore, taking items out of a relatively broad benefit package (known in the insurance literature as "delisting") is far more difficult politically than introducing new items into a relatively narrow benefit package. It is also a matter of some debate as to what the "basic" package should include. There are those who argue it should focus on financially catastrophic expenses, since this is why insurance is needed. Against this, it is often noted that this creates an incentive for people to postpone seeking care until they are very sick, thereby raising the cost of care; this points to including prevention and basic care in the package. Controversy abounds, too, over what a supplementary package might include. Should it cover copayments incurred for the basic package? Some countries outlaw such a practice on the grounds that it undermines the idea of copayments. Should it include certain interventions not covered by the basic package? Some argue against this on equity grounds, though this objection might be overcome by making the supplementary package free to the poor and other Decision 139 beneficiaries.

Should the supplementary package focus on amenities, such as allowing a patient the choice of surgeon, or the option of being treated in a private hospital? If so, does it need to be made available free to Decision 139 beneficiaries?

A less controversial strategy for VSS in its efforts to contain costs would be to pay providers in such a way as to encourage cost consciousness, for example, by shifting from FFS to a case-based payment system in paying for inpatient care. Such efforts are unlikely to reduce the number of inpatient admissions or outpatient department visits (indeed one would need to be careful not to encourage them), but rather to reduce the cost per admission and the cost per visit by discouraging tests and other items of care that generate revenues for the provider (each brings additional revenue because they constitute a separate service item), even if there is no medical case for delivering them. VSS would be more successful in this regard if supply-side subsidies were shifted to the demand side, and if out-of-pocket payments were reduced. Then VSS becomes the main, if not sole, payer of hospitals, and this "monopsony" status provides it with considerable leverage over providers. This leverage would be greater if it is allowed to selectively contract (it could choose from which providers its members could get care), if it can contract with public *and* private providers (this becomes more viable if supply-side subsidies are reduced and are not creating a tilted "playing field" between public and private providers), and if there is some role for VSS and providers to negotiate over the amount of the case-based payment. The latter process need not be a free-for-all. The Health Ministry could set guidelines for case-based payment rates for different case types, and the negotiated rate could be required to be within, say, plus or minus 10 percent of the guideline rate. These issues are discussed further in chapter 6.

With VSS financing the lion's share of providers' costs for the bulk of the population, it would have much greater leverage to bring about cost reductions by curbing the delivery of unnecessary care. Linked to the shift from FFS toward other payment methods would need to be the development of capacity within VSS to monitor and incentivize the delivery of *appropriate* health care. Care that is simply inappropriate, and hence ineffective, would need weeding out, but so, too, would care that is not cost-effective, especially where treatments are used for which a cheaper and equally effective treatment is available. VSS would also want to look at how care is delivered, ensuring, for example, that relatively sophisticated care is delivered by clinical teams that are specialized, rather than having all providers deliver all possible interventions. One strategy for VSS to promote good-quality health care would be to require that providers follow clinical guidelines.

The "clinical pathway" is an attractive way of operationalizing clinical guidelines. For a given clinical condition, the pathway spells out what steps need to be taken on each day for a typical case. The medical staff, having taken the appropriate step, signs the pathway document. If deviations are required, they need to be justified. A copy of the pathway can be made available to the patient, which has the merit of making the patient feel more confident that the treatment decisions are based only on medical considerations. More important from the financial perspective is that a copy can be supplied to the insurer or payer, which provides them with a tool to check the reasonableness of the provider's bills. The MOH has already begun exploring the pathways approach, and is planning a pilot scheme. The design of case-based payments could be linked to the pathway approach. From pathways, "normal" or "benchmark" costs could be calculated that reflect the resources required to treat patients optimally—not the resources currently used, which could be too many in cases where patients receive unnecessary tests and too much care, or too few when patients are discharged too early and "undertreated." Of course, it may be desirable to start with more generous diagnosis-related groups (DRGs), and only gradually reduce the DRG to the rate indicated by the pathway exercise. VSS has already started experimenting with DRGs, and the MOH has done some analytic work of its own.

CHAPTER 5

Service Delivery

The *Doi Moi* reforms of the 1980s started a process of considerable change among Vietnam's health providers. Budget support was cut, and facilities were allowed to charge patients directly, retain user fee revenues, and—subject to limits—use these revenues to pay staff (mostly through higher bonuses, but also through the hiring of contract staff). Amid concerns of health care becoming unaffordable, Vietnam put in place in the mid-1990s a set of fees and charges, in practice a mixture of per diem rates and fees per item of service. This schedule has remained largely intact ever since, although procedures that did not exist at the time have been priced in prevailing prices rather than 1995 prices, and the prices of drugs are not regulated. Only very limited attempts have been made to depart from this payment model—the MOH and the insurance agency have independently been exploring the use of diagnosis-related groups. The most recent reform initiative took the form of Decree 10—revised and given even more "teeth" in Decree 43—which required that service delivery units (SDUs) across the whole of government become more self-sufficient financially. SDUs have been encouraged to earn more income from clients and to use these extra revenues to pay higher salaries to staff, with the presumption being among commentators that budget support will be scaled back even further in due course.

This chapter outlines the key features of Vietnam's health delivery system, and goes on to present the limited available data on performance. It finds that the quality of care for mothers and small children seems to have improved, and is good by international standards, although one pair of surveys suggests that in the specific area of pneumonia treatment, Vietnam's quality of care deteriorated in the 1990s. Data confirm that costs in the hospital sector are rising rapidly, and that the bulk of the annual increase *cannot* be explained by increases in throughput. The increasingly costly style of care seems likely to be caused by providers having an incentive to deliver tests and drugs whose prices are either not regulated or are regulated, but at a rate that is generous by the standards of the 1995 schedule. The chapter then goes on to explain the intricacies of Decrees 10 and 43. It looks at the factors explaining why it was adopted in some parts of the country and in some types of facilities more quickly than in others, and at its impact on hospitals' financial performance. It concludes that the changes have indeed encouraged hospitals to earn more user fee income, but that they have also raised costs, especially administrative costs. Nothing, regrettably, can be said with existing data about their impacts on the quality of care.

Institutional Background and Policy Makers' Concerns

The Public Sector

As discussed above, during the late 1980s and early to mid-1990s, the first *Doi Moi* decade, central government spending on hospitals was drastically reduced, limiting further expansion and resulting in falling per-capita hospital bed availability. Provinces became a major financing source for hospitals, drawing on fee and insurance revenues. Meanwhile, the thinking of the time, for example, as stated in the World Bank's *Growing Healthy* sector study (World Bank 2001), found that Vietnam had invested too much public money in the hospital sector and was overly reliant on hospitals for treatment, with inpatient admission rates above those for Malaysia and Thailand, but with benefits accruing disproportionately to upper-income strata. Also, many indications pointed to inefficiency in providing services, as well as quality standards that were well below acceptable levels.

The government responded to this syndrome of hospital overuse and bypassing commune health centers by enhancing support for preventive and primary care services. Directive No. 06-CT/TW of the

Executive Committee of the Communist Party of Vietnam set the direction for strengthening the grassroots health network by, among other things, "increasing human resources and equipment for the grassroots health care network." The prime minister's decision of June 1996 set guiding principles and goals in terms of health promotion as an essential feature in the development and implementation of health services. Meanwhile, the Ministry of Home Affairs (MHA) and MOH worked together to improve the quantity and quality of commune health workers (CHWs) and village health workers (VHWs).[18] Real health outlays rose in the 1990s, including higher spending on national family planning and disease control programs, and starting in 1994, direct funding for the salaries of CHC health workers. Improved supplies and affordability of drugs brought reductions in out-of-pocket health spending.

Still, after these and other steps, CHCs averaged only 12 visits a day in 1998, with the rate much lower in impoverished rural regions, while in urban areas in which insurance-based financing was more prevalent, many patients continued to bypass CHCs even as outpatients.

Meanwhile, robust gains were being recorded in a number of regions and for the whole country in various indicators of hospital use. The reality was that despite the management obstacles that stood in the way of overcoming chronic inefficiencies, hospitals are essential for a reasonable quality of life, and for some they were indispensable for survival itself. Such facilities were popular politically, in part because they provided a model and example of quality, and a source of technical support of training if organized and funded well. Finally, hospitals were key elements underpinning Vietnam's health insurance setup.

The health care system in Vietnam is organized according to administrative level, with the MOH exercising overall responsibility at the central level. The MOH also directly controls 49 institutions, including medical and pharmaceutical universities/schools, central hospitals, research institutes, and so forth. At the provincial level, every province (of about 1 million to 1.5 million people) has a provincial Department of Health (DOH), with overall responsibility for health care activities in the respective province. Under this DOH, there are a number of provincial general hospitals and specialty hospitals, and provincial preventive health centers. At the district level, each district (about 100,000 to 200,000 people) has a District Health Office, a district hospital, and a district preventive center, and some intercommunal polyclinics.

Vietnam's hospitals are numerous and diverse. In 2007, there were over 1,000 government-run and more than 40 privately owned and operated hospitals. In most parts of the country, hospitals remain significantly, highly, or even completely dependent on transfers from the central budget. As laid out in the 2004 Master Plan of the Hospital Network, Vietnam's government hospitals and other facilities fall into different functional and administrative levels:

- At the *commune level*, (7,000 to 12,000 people) there is a CHC with three to five health workers, normally including a medical doctor (70 percent of CHCs have one), an assistant doctor, a midwife, and a nurse. The CHC is the basic level of health care in the public system and responsible for the primary level of care, including preventive care, normal delivery, provision of drugs, family planning, and overall health promotion in the community. Each village is expected to have one or two VHWs to provide basic health care services, including the expanded program on immunization (EPI) campaign, health education and communication, etc. The VHWs are particularly significant for extending health care services in poor and remote areas and in ethnic minority communities.

- At the *district level*, there are intercommune clinics and district hospitals/polyclinics, all of which admit inpatients, and provide emergency care and basic treatment for common diseases. On average, the almost 600 district-level hospitals have fewer than 80 beds (MOH 2000), and vary widely in technical sophistication and quality of services.

- At the *provincial level*, some 324 specialized and general hospitals treat diseases that are beyond the capability of the district hospitals or require "special treatment." Province hospitals (including large city hospitals) are administered by the provincial health departments. Ranging from 300 to 500 beds, province hospitals are significantly larger than district hospitals and provide curative and outpatient needs of both local and regional populations. Central-level, specialized, and general hospitals under MOH management provide highly specialized treatment with advanced techniques. These are the largest and most technically up-to-date facilities, with an average of over 500 beds. Almost all are located in Vietnam's largest cities.

Hospitals vary according to their accessibility. The rural/urban population ratio is highly positively correlated with the district/provincial bed ratio, implying that the more rural the province, the greater the reliance on district hospitals. In mountainous regions, such as the northeast and northwest, there are a higher number of district hospitals per million population. In these areas, district hospitals are important because they provide an alternative to hard-to-reach provincial center. In other areas, even other rural areas such as the Mekong Delta region, there are comparatively fewer district hospitals despite a reasonably high reliance on them because of the ease of travel.

There are also large differences in the number of beds per capita across regions. The north central and Central Highlands regions suffer from far fewer beds per capita, and in particular, fewer provincial beds, than other regions. These two regions have among the lowest average incomes in the country, suggesting that the limitation might be on the demand side. In the Central Highlands, this appears to be the case, with occupancy rates in both district and provincial hospitals well below the national average. However, in the north central region, occupancy rates averaging 109 percent in provincial hospitals in 2004 indicate a supply of beds unable to keep up with demand.

Interestingly, the northwest region, with the lowest monthly income and the highest proportion of rural population, is well above average in terms of provincial and district beds per capita. Occupancy rates of 76 percent (compared with the national average of 94 percent) in district hospitals indicate that this may reflect an oversupply, at least with respect to the rest of the country. This reflects a focused campaign of the government to increase the number of beds in the region, but indicates that accessibility in some areas continues to be a problem. The Mekong Delta region in particular faces accessibility problems that are exacerbated by the network of canals and the frequent flooding.

Health observers in Vietnam have expressed concern that hospitals in rural areas find it difficult to attract qualified medical staff. The available evidence does not confirm these fears. However, there are a number of caveats for these statistics. Hospitals in rural areas don't appear to have significantly fewer qualified staff per bed or per inpatient day. However, these statistics don't give any indication as to whether rural areas suffer in terms of qualified staff per capita. Higher indirect costs of hospital use (resulting from high transport costs facing many rural residents) result in fewer admissions per capita in these areas. So while the hospitals in rural areas might have adequate levels of qualified staff when assessed in relation to the number of patients who manage to reach the hospital, the overall population still might not be adequately serviced by current staffing levels. Programs to improve ease of access to hospitals might create staffing shortages if this issue is not addressed. Hospitals in the rural category are far smaller (in terms of number of beds) than the more urban categories. Due to economies of scale 100 beds spread across a number of smaller hospitals will require more staff than the same number of beds in one hospital, so rural areas require a higher ratio of staff to beds than urban areas with much larger hospitals.

District hospitals in rural areas serve a different function from those in urban areas. They treat more seriously ill patients and have higher occupancy rates than those in urban areas (that compete with better equipped nearby provincial and central hospitals). The required levels of doctors, nurses, and specialists are therefore higher in these remote regions.

The Private Sector

The private sector appears to have grown considerably in recent years. Drug vendors are the biggest group, accounting for 18 percent of private "providers" in 1999, followed by general practitioner clinics (16 percent), traditional medicine clinics (14 percent), private pharmacies (14 percent), and nursing homes (12 percent); the private hospital sector, by contrast, is highly undeveloped (Government of Vietnam-Donor Working Group on Public Expenditure Review 2000). A recent study (Tuan et al. 2005) conducted in 30 of the 160 communes in the province of Hung Yen found almost twice as many private providers per 10,000 people (11.5) than public providers (6.7)—far more private providers than recorded in official documents. This reflects the fact that less than 20 percent of private providers had registered with the authorities. The study also found that the private sector treats more than two-thirds of all illnesses treated at the community level. This is, however, a small-scale study, and generalizing from it to the rest of Vietnam would be dangerous.

Provider Performance

The bulk of inpatient admissions occur at the hospital level, but an appreciable number (20 percent on average over the last 10 years) occur at the CHC level (figure 5.1). In contrast, outpatient visits occur more frequently at the CHC than the hospital level. However, the differential is not as large as might be expected: CHCs have seen only 1.6 times as many outpatients as hospitals, and while the differential has been growing, hospitals continue to be an important source of outpatient visits.

Hospitals have increased their outpatient visits and inpatient admissions by an average of 5 percent a year since 1998 (figure 5.1). In contrast, over the same period, inpatient admissions to CHCs fell, but recently began to increase. CHC outpatient visits, on the other hand, increased dramatically, averaging 13 percent growth per year. The recent years have seen the fastest growth of outpatient visits at the CHC level. According to MOH administrative data, outpatient consultation rates at the CHC level and above have reached nearly 0.30 per person per year. This is somewhat higher than the figure that emerges from the latest VHLSS household survey (0.25).

Vietnam's inpatient admission rate is not much different from that of developed countries, but its outpatient visit rate appears to be much lower (table 5.1), pointing to a health system that is heavily biased toward inpatient care. Its admission rate is also high given its

Figure 5.1: Trends in Inpatient Admissions and Outpatient Visits

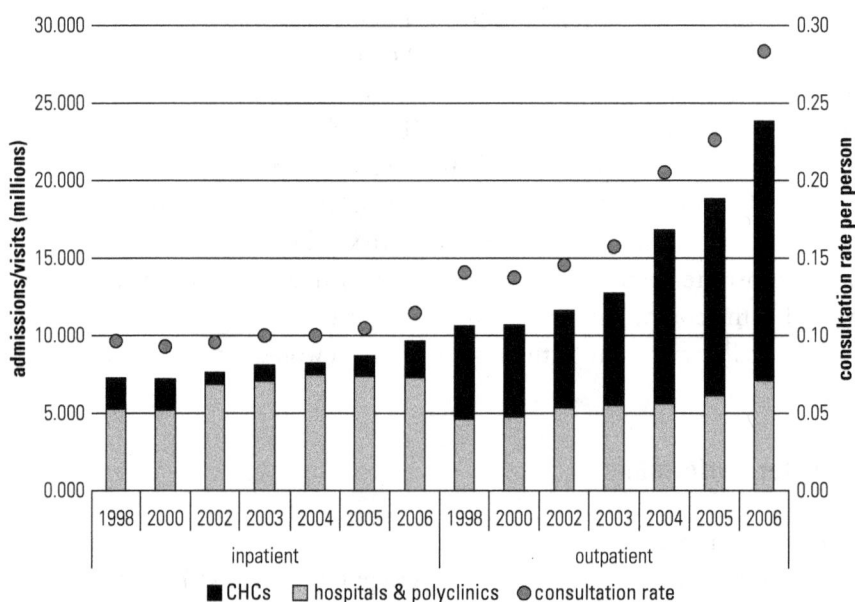

Source: MOH Health Statistics Yearbook, various years.

Table 5.1: Vietnam Inpatient and Outpatient Statistics in Context

	OUTPATIENT VISITS PER CAPITA	INPATIENT ADMISSIONS PER 100 PERSONS	AV. LENGTH OF STAY	HOSPITAL BEDS PER 10,000 PERSONS	BED OCCUPANCY RATE	DOCTORS PER 10,000 PERSONS
Hong Kong, China	8.3	14.0		51.8		15.8
Japan	16.0	9.6	37.3	129.4	0.8	20.2
Korea, Rep.	9.8	7.0	13.4	66.3	0.4	19.4
Singapore		12.0		28.2		15.0
Taiwan	8.4	9.0		59.2		14.0
OECD average	7.1	16.4	10.2	60.3	0.8	28.0
Vietnam						
Public hospital	0.1	8.7	11.6	15.9	1.7	
CHC	0.2	2.8		8.1		
All public	0.3	11.5	8.2	24.1	1.1	6.3

Source: Data from other countries except average length of stay from "Health systems in East Asia: what can developing countries learn from Japan and the Asian Tigers?" Data on outpatient visits and inpatient admissions from MOH Health Statistics Yearbook, and are for 2006. Data on average length of stay for countries other than Vietnam are from OECD health database. Data from Vietnam are computed from hospital inventory for hospitals and refers to 2004; figure for "all public" is from Growing Healthy and is for 1998. Data on hospital beds are from Government Statistical Office Web site and are for 2005. Bed occupancy rate for all countries is computed from the figures on inpatient admissions, beds per 10,000 and average length of stay. Bed occupancy rate from hospital inventory is 92%.

Table 5.2: Changes in Service Delivery, 1997–2002 from DHS

VARIABLE	1997	2002	CHANGE	T-STAT
Services (max 4) offered by local private doctor	0.517	0.854	0.067	3.04
Private pharmacy in commune	0.527	0.668	0.028	2.93
Public pharmacy in commune	0.360	0.244	−0.023	−2.56
Beds in CHC	8.104	5.639	−0.493	−2.75
Outpatients in CHC	19.095	18.707	−0.077	−0.05
Medical staff in CHC	4.754	5.322	0.114	1.66
Items (max 27) in stock/ available in CHC	15.227	17.400	0.435	8.18
Services (max 5) offered by CHC	4.128	4.488	0.072	3.24
Medicines (max 8) available in CHC	5.567	6.488	0.184	6.35
Beds in nearest health center (not CHC)	74.262	85.211	2.190	1.05
Outpatients in nearest health center (not CHC)	156.180	152.919	−0.652	−0.07
Medical staff in nearest health center (not CHC)	52.478	74.795	4.463	3.37
Items (max 27) in stock/ available in nearest health center (not CHC)	17.473	19.839	0.473	3.16
Services (max 5) offered by nearest health center (not CHC)	3.271	3.771	0.100	2.77
Medicines (max 8) available in nearest health center (not CHC)	5.532	6.327	0.159	3.07

Source: Tabulations from DHS.

bed stock: when calculated the same way as for the developed countries in table 5.1, its bed-occupancy rate is well over 100 percent. This may reflect the fact that the beds recorded in the ministry's data are "planned" beds—the figure used in budget allocations—since the bed occupancy rate that emerges from the hospital inventory database is around 90 percent. Still, even this is high by international standards, and in the hospital inventory there are many hospitals with rates in excess of 100 percent. It is likely—but there are, it seems, no data to confirm this—that in Vietnam, many inpatient admissions could have been avoided, at least in part, through high-quality outpatient care, which is lacking in Vietnam.

The health facility modules of the 1997 and 2002 Demographic and Health Surveys (DHS) shed light on other changes in Vietnam's health facilities, at both commune and district levels (table 5.2). Bed stocks were reduced over the period 1997–2002 at the CHC level, but increased at the district hospital level. Staff numbers increased at both levels, but especially at the district level. Both CHCs and district hospitals increased the number of stocked items and services relevant to maternal and child health—common indirect measures of quality in the first level of care in developing countries. Despite these changes, the number of outpatients seen at both the CHC level and at the district level did not, according to the DHS data, change over the period. This is not consistent with the MOH administrative data, which even in this period showed some increase.

In Vietnam, as in many—if not most—other countries, very little routine data are collected that shed light on the quality of care. Limited—and very dated—evidence on quality is available from health facility surveys undertaken by WHO that focus on care administered to small children (World Health Organization 1998). Children with diarrhea appear to receive care that is high quality by international standards (figure 5.2). A high fraction of children with

Figure 5.2: Quality of Care to Children with Diarrhea, Late 1990s

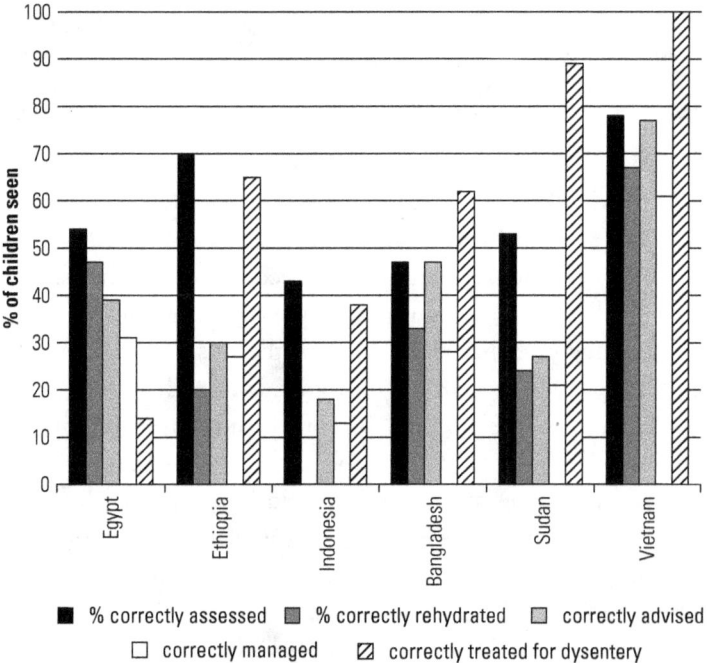

Source: WHO.

diarrhea are correctly assessed, and a high fraction of these are correctly rehydtrated. High fractions of caregivers with such children were also correctly advised and the children's treatment was correctly managed in a high proportion of cases. A full 100 percent of children with dysentery were treated correctly. The picture is less impressive as far as children presenting with pneumonia are concerned (figure 5.3). Vietnam scored well in the first survey, undertaken in 1993, but much poorer in the second survey, undertaken in 1995.

The aforementioned study (Tuan et al. 2005) of the private and public sectors in Hung Yen province also sheds light on the quality of care in the two sectors. It found that 11 percent of private sector providers had no medical qualifications, and that while patients were just as satisfied with private providers as with public ones, the quality of care—measured in terms of equipment and availability of supplies, as well as clinic performance and skills—was inferior in the private sector, though by no means perfect in the public sector.

Figure 5.3: Quality of Care to Children with Pneumonia, Late 1990s

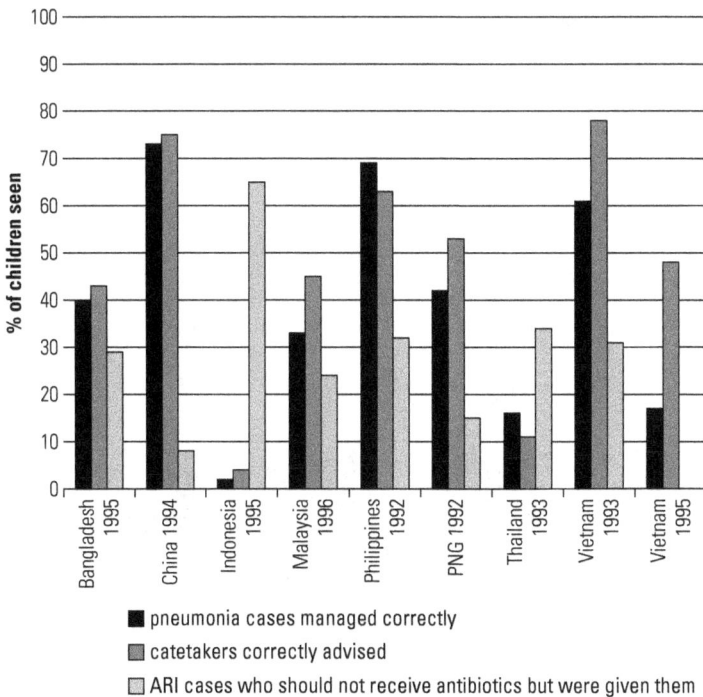

Source: WHO.

What of the cost of health care in Vietnam? The same Hung Yen study sheds some light on this issue. It finds that the cost of private sector care (inclusive of drug costs) is eight times that in Delhi, India. No comparisons have been undertaken of the cost of publicly provided health in Vietnam and elsewhere. But what is clear is that the cost of care—at least at the hospital level for which data are available—is rising rapidly (figure 5.4). In 2004–05, hospital costs rose by 21 percent. Average costs (cost per case) have also been increasing, though not by as much.

Two questions can be asked of the cost increases. The first is: How far can they be explained in terms of increased activity and increased complexity of case mix? In other words, how far are they explained by throughput changes? The second is: What components of cost have risen quickest? In other words, looking from an accounting perspective, which items of expenditure have risen most quickly?

Addressing the first question, part of the increase in total costs is indeed due to increased numbers of outpatients and inpatients. These increased by 7 percent and 6 percent, respectively, between 2004 and 2005. Hospitals also delivered more diagnostic tests over this period (x-rays per patient increased by 5 percent, and ultra-

Figure 5.4: Hospital Cost Inflation

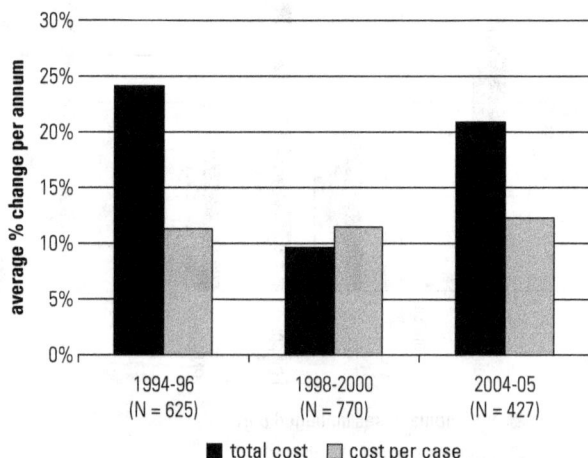

■ total cost ▨ cost per case

Source: Calculations from Vietnam hospital inventory.

sounds per patient by 7 percent), undertook more surgery (the number of surgical cases per patient increased by 3 percent), and delivered more procedures per patient (a rise of 5 percent). But exactly how far can the cost increases be attributed to increases in throughput and case mix? Figure 5.5 gives the answer. It decomposes[19] the rise in hospital costs into two parts: an "explained" part, reflecting increased throughput (more inpatients and outpatients), a more complex case mix (more surgery, procedures, and diagnostic tests per patient), and additional beds, and an "unexplained" part. Only 8.4 percentage points of the 21 percent increase in hospital costs between 2004 and 2005 is "explained." Of this, the bulk (5.5 percentage points) is attributable to more cases being treated. Just 2 percentage points is due to a more complex case mix. The majority (13 percentage points) of the 21

Figure 5.5: Breaking Down Hospital Cost Inflation

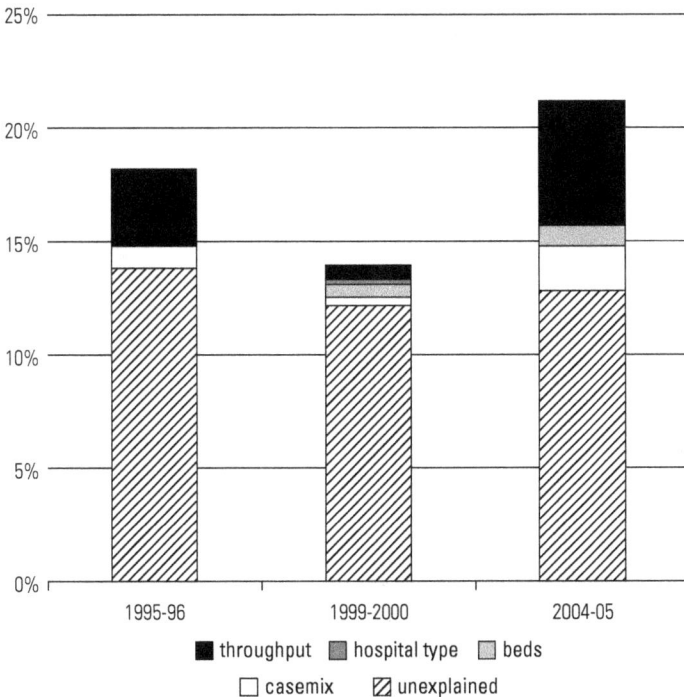

Source: Calculations from Vietnam hospital inventory.

percent increase in cost is "unexplained," meaning that hospital patients on average cost 13 percent more to treat in 2005 than in 2004, *even adjusting for the fact that the 2005 case mix was more complex than that of 2004* (there were more surgery cases per patient, more diagnostic tests per patient, and more procedures per patient). In all years—but especially 1999–2000—increased throughput and case mix complexity account for a very small part of the observed increase in hospital costs (figure 5.5).

What about the second question—the accounting perspective on cost increases? It turns out that it is largely wage costs that have been driving hospital cost increases (table 5.3). Roughly half of the growth is accounted for by wage increases, although wages make up only 40 percent of total costs. Rising drug costs account for 30 percent of the increase in total costs.

Table 5.3: An Accounting Breakdown of Cost Increases, 1999–2000

	SHARE 1999	GROWTH 1999–2000	CONTRIBUTION TO GROWTH 1999–2000
Cost	100%	17%	14.5%
Salaries	20%	20%	3.8%
Overtime	5%	35%	1.5%
Surgery allowance	2%	4%	0.1%
Hazard and risk allowance	1%	18%	0.2%
Incentives and bonuses	13%	19%	2.4%
Electricity costs	3%	8%	0.3%
Water costs	1%	24%	0.2%
Fuel costs	1%	19%	0.2%
Drug costs	26%	17%	4.3%
Blood costs	1%	14%	0.2%
Laboratory & chemical costs	3%	24%	0.8%
X-ray film costs	1%	−38%	−0.8%
Consumables costs	2%	−1%	0.0%
Medical consultation costs	5%	−5%	−0.3%
Repairs & maintenance costs	3%	1%	0.0%
Fixed asset costs	6%	0%	0.0%
Training costs	0%	19%	0.1%
Other costs	8%	22%	1.7%

Source: Tabulations from hospital inventory 2004–05.

Prices and Provider Payment

Part of the explanation for the growth in volume of care delivered and the growth of unit costs lies in the way providers are paid in Vietnam. They receive their income from three main sources: the budget (still the largest source of revenue), out-of-pocket payments by patients, and income from the health insurance agency, VSS. During the last 10 years or so, among hospitals, the budget has steadily shrunk as a source of revenue, and health insurance income has increased (figure 5.6). The share of revenues from user fees increased somewhat between 1998 and 2000, but then fell back. Since both fee-paying patients and VSS pay providers on a FFS basis, there has been, in effect, a gradual shift away from budgets toward FFS in the hospital sector, albeit with a third-party

Figure 5.6: Source of Hospital Revenues, Vietnam 1998–2005

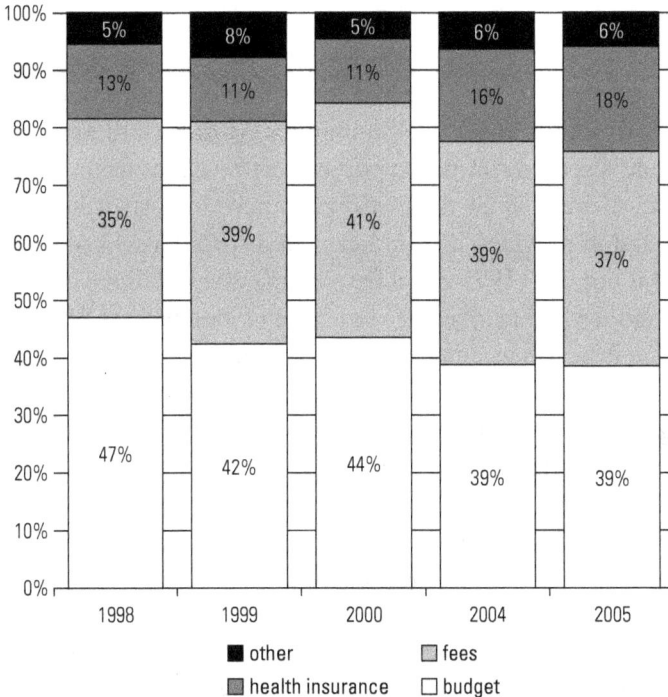

Source: Calculations from Vietnam hospital inventory.

payer growing in importance. What figure 5.6 does not show is informal payments—these add to the official payments, and increase the share of out-of-pocket payments. In the system as a whole, as seen in the previous chapter, the share of health expenditures financed through out-of-pocket payments is almost twice as large as the share of government hospital costs financed through out-of-pocket spending. One factor explaining the discrepancy is the fact that out-of-pocket payments in the National Health Accounts total expenditure figure include payments to private facilities (including drug vendors).

Out-of-pocket payments by patients were seen initially as a temporary solution to the problem of falling government revenues that marked the early days of *Doi Moi*. The consequent budget cuts represented an administrative challenge to the government, since the government's control of flows of allocated funds was seen as crucial for "enforcing" direct management of hospitals, in effect as MOH departments. Once budgets fell, new administrative instruments were needed. Some saw user fees as quasiadministrative tools. But user fees were not suited to the task. One disadvantage was the direct and immediate impact they had on utilization—poverty considerations had to be factored in, at minimum. Moreover, there were considerable disparities in the importance of revenues from fees across regions. Generally, fee revenues were more important in wealthier areas, and in province-level rather than district-level hospitals.

It was not until 1995 that a fee schedule was published. A methodology was devised to arrive at a structure of fees that was "efficient" in bringing in revenues, improving hospital quality and the accessibility of public medical care services, as well as targeting public subsidies to changing incentives and utilization patterns. An interministerial commission consisting of representatives from MOH, the Ministry of Finance (MOF), the Ministry of Labor, War Invalids, and Social Affairs (MOLISA) and the State Price Commission (SPC) was to establish a range of fees, drawing on technical support from MOH staff. The latter would propose a fee range that had been reviewed by facility administrators, and staff from MOF and SPC. The proposal and reviews were forwarded to the commission, which then issued interministerial circulars listing the range of fees that was permissible.

In 1993, the commission staff put before the commission a proposal to update health care prices, which was accepted.[20]

The fees in the schedule are a mixture of per-item charges (for example., for tests) and per diem rates (e.g. for inpatient stays), with ranges for each type, and variations according to the type of hospital (higher class hospitals being able to charge more). Except for a few minor changes, fees have been unchanged since the major initiative of 1995, not even to adjust for inflation. Interventions that did not exist in 1995 have been added to the list, at the prevailing price. Drugs are not included in the list of fees. Hospitals negotiate drug prices with pharmaceutical companies, and pass on the costs to the patient or VSS, with little oversight or regulation from MOH. According to a recent MOH study, fees cover only 39 percent to 71 percent of the average costs of treating seven common conditions (such as pneumonia, Caesarean section appendicitis, stroke, and intracranial injury).

FFS in general gives providers an incentive to increase volume, even if this means delivering services of questionable necessity. But it also gives providers an incentive to focus on interventions that are more profitable. In the case of Vietnam, this means items covered by the fee schedule that have been added since 1995, and drugs that are not covered by the price schedule. Insofar as the interventions covered by the 1995 price schedule are relatively low tech, and hospitals are able to charge higher fees for high-tech services, we would expect to see hospitals drifting toward a more high-tech and high-cost style of care. This would explain why the rising numbers of cases explains so little of the rapid increase in hospital costs in Vietnam. Vietnam's payment system is also likely to encourage providers to focus on case types requiring tests and other interventions that are priced favorably, and on case types where a high fraction of the cost is comprised of drugs. In both instances, providers can recover a larger fraction of the costs of care through payments by patients or VSS. A recent study shows that in the case of pneumonia in children, only 39 percent of provider costs are covered by allowable fees, while 71 percent of the cost of treating intracranial injuries is. An unscrupulous hospital manager might be tempted to encourage physicians to focus on treating patients with intracranial injuries rather than children suffering from pneumonia.

The continued emphasis on budgets also creates undesirable incentives. Budgets are based on the number of "planned" beds (the hospital's official number of beds), which gives hospitals a strong incentive to use their beds (or at least report them as being used) in order to protect their budgets (AusAID Study Team 2007). The high occupancy rates reported in the MOH data (averaging in excess of 100 percent since 2000) partly reflect this incentive. Hospitals have every incentive to fill beds with cases that could be treated at a lower level in the system, or on a day-case or ambulatory basis. Higher-level hospitals are the ones with the highest occupancy rates. Like the lower-level hospitals with lower occupancy rates, they hope that high occupancy rates will result in an upward adjustment of their planned bed numbers, and hence an upward revision of their budgets. In the competition for beds, higher-level hospitals have the advantage of being perceived by patients as offering higher-quality care.

Autonomy

A key aspect of service delivery is autonomy. Some aspects of autonomy have already been mentioned. *Doi Moi* permitted providers to supplement their budgets with user charges. Their fees are fixed by the aforementioned fee schedule, but drugs prices are not regulated (though they are monitored), and providers have the scope, in practice, to levy unofficial charges. As already mentioned, too, providers have very limited autonomy when it comes to inputs. They are restricted by bed norms. They are also restricted in their capital spending by capital budgets that are norm based. Low capital budgets and low equipment maintenance allowances have led to old and poorly maintained equipment, much of which is obsolete. Hand in hand with bed norms go staff norms that restrict a hospital's ability to change its skills mix, and alter its staffing level. Basic salaries are also fixed, with little variation geographically, by seniority or by specialty. Incentive payments are, however, permitted, though were restricted prior to recent reforms by Decree 33/1995, which stipulated that staff be entitled to 30 percent of the gross revenues from user fees, with the other 70 percent to be used for recurrent spending.

Incentive payments have inevitably been larger in facilities with a healthy balance sheet. The effect has been to encourage doctors and other medical staff to try to work in such facilities, creating imbalances in the system—between rural areas and urban areas, for example. In addition to their ability to retain a portion of financial surpluses to supplement their basic salaries, providers in Vietnam enjoy unlimited freedom in their clinical decision making. No clinical guidelines exist, let alone ones that are enforced by the MOH or VSS, and there is no credible quality assurance mechanism. Providers are largely free to treat patients as they choose.

Arguably, then, in areas where providers ought to face at least some restrictions in their decision making—clinical decisions, the setting of prices for drugs, the ability to benefit financially from higher hospital revenues, and so on—providers have enjoyed a high degree of autonomy. In contrast, in areas where it makes good sense for them to have more latitude—the number of beds in the facility, the skill mix, and so forth—they have not.

Decrees 10/2002 and 43/2006 (the latter replaced the former) altered certain aspects of provider autonomy in Vietnam (table 5.4). The two decrees confer upon hospitals increased discretion over financial operations, management of human resources, organization of services, and choices of services offered. In essence, hospitals will play a much greater, more direct, and formally sanctioned role in shaping the costs, qualities, and distribution of services at the point of delivery.

Decrees 10 and 43 differ from previous user fee policies in that they align the incentives of providers (hospital staff) with the overall financial performance of the health facility. Compared to the old user fee policy in Decree 33/1995, Decree 10 promises a bigger potential income for the staff, although with caps on the maximum allowances and bonuses, and further that these are based on net revenues (revenues from user fees, minus recurrent expenditures). Thus, as it were, the hospital staff members are residual claimants. However, Decree 10 does not make it easy for the hospital staff to claim their part of the income residual. The net revenue is divided into two parts: (a) three funds for staff benefits; and (b) a fund for facility upgrades. The three staff funds do not, however, provide outright

Table 5.4: Decrees 10 and 43 Compared

	DECREE 10	DECREE 43
Objective	To grant financial autonomy to all revenue-raising public service entities (including hospitals) that recover their recurrent expenditures fully or partially	To grant financial autonomy to all revenue-raising public service entities that recover full, part, or none of their recurrent expenditures, and to other special public entities and their branches
Cost management	−Set management and operating expenditure norms −Assign and manage staff, hire temporary workers, set level of wages and allowances according to guidelines −Determine recurrent and capital expenditures	−Set management and operating expenditure norms for all units −Establish, merge, or dismantle subordinate units −Determine the size, composition, and assignment of permanent staff, hire temporary workers, set level of wages and allowances according to guidelines −Determine recurrent and capital expenditures −Adjust budget across expenditure items
Revenue management	−Open bank accounts, borrow or mobilize capital, tax reductions and exemptions −Determine the uses of all revenues, but restrictions apply on state budget	−Open bank accounts, borrow capital, tax reductions and exemptions −Determine uses of all revenues, but restrictions apply on state budget −Right to set user fees
Accountability	−Propose annual budget to PCOMs −Submit annual financial reports to relevant state agencies	−Propose annual budget to PCOMs −Submit annual financial reports to relevant state agencies
Allocation of net revenues (less recurrent expenditures)	−Staff gets the first cut (from contributions to income stabilization fund, bonus award funds, and welfare funds) −Wage increases less than 2.5 of basic for full-recovery agencies, and less than 2 of basic for partial-recovery agencies −Remaining amount goes to Public Service Development Fund (from capital investments)	−First 25% goes to development funds (for capital expenditures) −Then income supplements and contributions to the Staff Reward Fund; caps and other restrictions apply to firms that recover only a part or none of their recurrent expenditures

income supplements—they are intended to stabilize income in the event of a reduction in revenues, to reward individual performance, and to provide emergency support in cases where staff experience unforeseen changes to their financial circumstances.

Decree 43 sharpens the incentives of the providers, and at the same time ensures both the continued operation and the scope for upgrading the facility. The first 25 percent of net revenues are set aside for facility upgrading. Hospital staff then gets an outright share (in terms of additional income) of the remaining 75 percent. The levels of additional income, bonuses, and allowances are to be decided by the hospital director, presumably based on individual or group performance. If there are still net revenues left, these are contributed to the same staff funds specified in Decree 10.

To raise enough net revenues, Decree 10 grants the hospital director powers to manage the costs and revenues of the facility. The hospital director can set the expenditure norms, including the wages and allowances of staff—easily the biggest component of recurrent spending. The hospital can also be operated like a state-owned enterprise with its own seal and bank account, can mobilize or borrow capital, and avail itself of tax perks. The hospital director is given full day-to-day executive powers, subject only to the budget oversight of the local People's Committee, and the financial review of relevant state agencies. Decree 43 grants more power to hospital directors to reduce costs and raise revenues. A hospital director now has full control over manpower—hiring, firing, promotion, assignments—and subordinate units (create, merge, dismantle, etc.). The director can also set fees within a band. Another feature of Decree 43 that makes it more appealing to the hospital sector than Decree 10 is that it is applicable also to health facilities that are not able to recover any of their recurrent costs through user fee revenues. The staff members in these facilities are likewise entitled to income supplements, although with caps on the maximum.

Speed of Adoption of Decrees 10 and 43

The rollout of Decree 10 took time, in part due to the lack of hospital management capacity, but also because of MOH concerns about adverse impacts on patients and the availability of personnel in understaffed lower-level hospitals. Provincial hospitals were more likely to become autonomous earlier than district and central hospitals (figure 5.7). Variations are also evident across regions, with the Red River Delta being the fastest adopter (figure 5.8). A more thorough econometric analysis reveals that hospital type and region are indeed

Figure 5.7: Variations in Speed of Adoption of Decree 10 by Type of Hospital

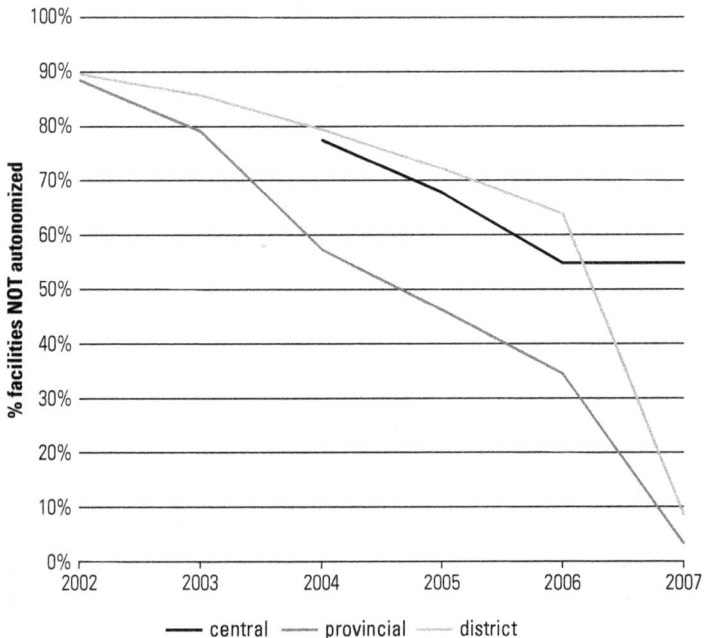

Source: Calculations from data provided by MOH.

the main drivers of the speed of autonomization. Provincial hospitals have a higher chance of adopting early. There are also differences across provinces in the speed of adoption. Among variables that can be measured, only GDP per capita emerges as a significant influence, with the unexpected result that richer provinces are *slower* to adopt.

Impacts of Decrees 10 and 43

Decrees 10 and 43 made hospitals more autonomous in areas where it was argued above their autonomy was inappropriately circumscribed—for example, human resource and other input decisions. However, they have either left unchecked or have increased still further providers' autonomy in areas where it was argued earlier they already enjoy too high a degree of autonomy—clinical decision making, price setting, the ability to benefit financially from higher hospital revenues, and so forth.

Figure 5.8: Variations in Speed of Adoption of Decree 10 by Type of Region

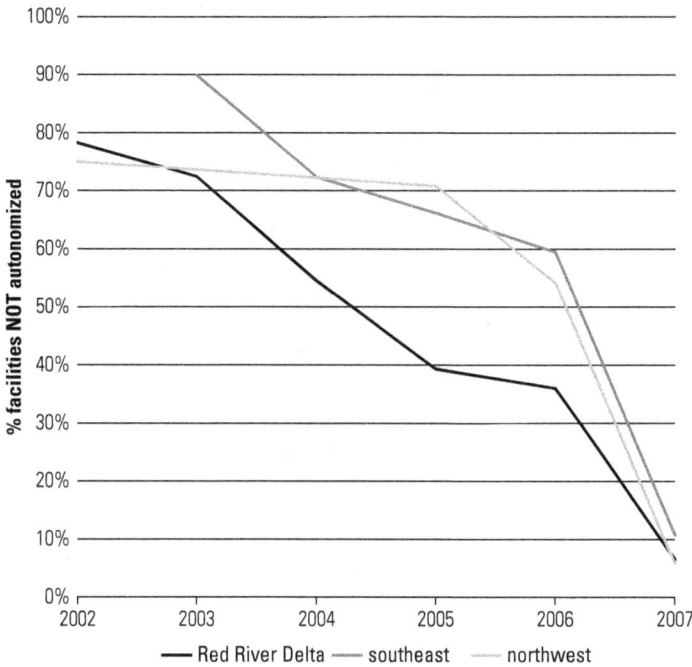

Source: Calculations from data provided by MOH.

The greater decision-making powers in areas such as capital, beds, and human resources are important advances and ought to provide much needed flexibility to Vietnam's hospital sector. There is, however, a risk that the flexibility will be exploited inappropriately in the pursuit of higher revenues and lower costs. The scope to set prices within a band is likely to lead to higher prices in areas where the public can afford the higher prices or where there is little competition, threatening the poor (and middle-income groups in areas where providers enjoy a monopoly) with unaffordable health care. The decrees give providers an incentive to focus still more on services and interventions that are profitable, and do nothing to change the incentive to strive for high-quality care except insofar as patients can recognize good-quality care and reward providers who deliver it with strong recommendations to friends and family. In all likelihood, high tech will be confused with high quality, and since these are also more profitable interventions, the result of the decrees seems likely to be an "arms race" for medical technology and an even greater proliferation of unnecessary care.

Is there any evidence of any of this happening in practice? A preliminary evaluation of the effects of Decrees 10 and 43 was undertaken for this report, focusing specifically on the impacts on hospitals' financial performance. Rather than simply compare hospitals that have been autonomized with ones that have not, we estimate the impact of the program in a way that allows the impact to depend on how many years a hospital has been autonomous. It is not unreasonable to think that the impact may start quite small, and then grow as a hospital becomes used to its newfound autonomy and starts making changes. The analysis also allows for hospital-specific time-invariant unobservable factors that may influence the outcomes of interest *and* the timing of autonomization; this is made possible through the use of panel data. We have data for each hospital for both 2004 and 2005, and see, in effect, how the *growth* of costs between 2004 and 2005 is affected by whether the hospital has been autonomized and for how long.[21]

Provincial hospitals were the first to become autonomous under Decrees 10 and 43, and we would expect to see the largest impacts there. This is precisely what we find—indeed, we find no impacts at the district level. Autonomization leads to higher fee income for provincial hospitals, with the impact higher in the second year after adoption, and higher still in the third year. Autonomization makes for 47 percent higher out-of-pocket fee income *per case* by the third year. What these results do not tell us, of course, is how far the extra fee income can be justified by extra needed health care. The data do not allow this issue to be investigated. The analysis also reveals that these extra revenues come at a cost—administrative costs are substantially increased by autonomization, with administrative costs *per case* being double by the fourth year of autonomous status. There is also evidence that Decrees 10 and 43 increased other costs, though the impact is statistically significant only in the year after autonomization.

CHAPTER 6

Reforming Service Delivery

The successes of Vietnam's health care delivery system must be acknowledged. The tiered structure reaching down to the commune level has helped ensure broad coverage of preventive interventions and access to basic curative interventions for the bulk of the population. Much of the population has been able to access more advanced curative care as well. The system continues to treat more patients, especially at the outpatient level. The delivery system and the increased use of it almost certainly deserve some—if not much—of the credit for the impressive recent achievements in reducing mortality at all ages, and for bringing age-adjusted mortality rates on par with those of Malaysia, a much richer country. Exactly how much is due to the health system is, of course, hard to say.

But the system does face some challenges. Costs have been rising rapidly—far faster than can be explained by increased throughput. There are growing concerns about the quality of care and whether all care delivered is actually medically necessary. The rapid growth of costs owes much to the perverse incentives caused by the mixture of budgets and FFS. Budgets, being based on bed norms, encourage hospitals to jealously guard their bed stock and put patients in beds even if they could be treated at a lower level or on an outpatient basis. FFS encourages them to deliver more services, whether or not they are medically necessary. The health insurance agency VSS plays a very limited role as an informed "purchaser" of health services: it acts largely as a passive payer of bills, and in any case picks up only 13 percent of total health expenditures. Supply-side subsidies in the form of state budgets are also paid in a passive way, in line with bed norms. Neither VSS nor the state exercises much financial control over providers. Nor do they have measures in place to assure the quality of care. Patients are thus left largely to fend for themselves. But patients are poor "consumers" when it comes to health care because of their limited knowledge of medical matters. The scope for providers to induce demand for unnecessary care is high when they are paid on a FFS basis and are given strong incentives to generate revenues. Yet this is precisely the direction in which Decrees 10 and 43 have pushed the sector.

Delivery Reform Depends on Insurance Reform

Reforming the delivery system with the aim of driving down costs and driving up quality is a major challenge facing the government. How the system is best reformed depends crucially on the future development of the health insurance system.

At one extreme is a scenario where coverage expands toward 100 percent and there is a policy commitment that VSS will pick up a large fraction of the cost of care. In this scenario, supply-side subsidies could be largely redirected to the demand side in the form of greater tax-financed revenues for VSS. In this scenario, VSS would exert a significant leverage over providers. It would have a strong incentive and a mandate to develop a more rational payment system for providers, as well as a quality assurance mechanism that would in itself help to lower costs by curbing unnecessary care. Patients would no longer be left to fend for themselves, and the demand side of the health system that providers would deal with would be VSS rather than individual patient-consumers.

At the other extreme is the status quo. VSS would cover less than half of the population and an even smaller share of total health spending. VSS would be a minor payer of health care bills in Vietnam, and would lack the leverage, incentive, or mandate to develop new payment methods and quality assurance mechanisms. These tasks would fall to MOH. Supply-side subsidies would need to continue in order to keep out-of-pocket payments down for the uninsured. MOH could make progress on the quality assurance front, and these efforts could be of value to VSS. Payment reform could still occur. MOH could, for example, develop a case-based payment system for hospitals, and this could apply for all patients, insured and uninsured. MOH could pick up a given percentage of the case-based payment for all cases (including insured ones) from the state budget. Uninsured patients would pay the rest—perhaps 60 percent to 70 percent of the full amount, given the current financing flows. Insured patients would split the portion not covered by MOH with VSS; VSS might pick up 15 percent to 20 percent of the total cost, given its current revenues. Or the state budget could be focused entirely on uninsured patients, reducing out-of-pocket payments for this group. VSS and the insured would be left to split the entire amount of the case-based payment between them. This would raise out-of-pocket payments among the insured, unless VSS were able to raise revenues to cover the extra costs.

The second scenario suffers from providers facing too many payers, and the limited influence in terms of expenditures of the two third-party payers, MOH and VSS. Payment reform in this scenario is likely to be messier and less effective. The same is likely to be true of quality assurance reform, which without the financial leverage of a single payer is unlikely to have much "bite" with providers. A key element, therefore, to any strategy of improving provider performance must involve moving to a single-payer model. In Vietnam's context, this means ensuring that VSS covers not only the bulk of the population, but also the bulk of health care expenditures.

Of course, this approach will be more effective the more effective VSS is as a payer and purchaser. It will take time for VSS to move from its present role as a passive payer of bills. It cannot do this alone—the quality enhancement and payment tools discussed below will need to be developed by several parts of government jointly—but the success of the venture will depend a great deal on how far VSS will invest in its capacity to use these tools effectively.

Improving the Quality of Care

Clinical guidelines have the potential to improve quality of care for inpatients and ambulatory care patients. But they also have the potential to reduce costs by curbing unnecessary care. For this to happen, there must be incentives for providers to follow the guidelines. If following guidelines means losing revenue, providers are unlikely to follow them. "Carrots" and "sticks" can both be used. The obvious "stick" is to reduce payments to providers who do not adhere to the guidelines. This is more easily done in the first scenario above, where there is one payer, VSS. If VSS can detect noncompliance with the guidelines, it could reduce the payment to the provider for the case. In the scenario where VSS, MOH, and patients themselves all pay some money to the provider, the issue arises of who will identify noncompliance. Patients, as the biggest payer, have the strongest incentive, but they are in the weakest position to do so. They could take their case to an ombudsman who is authorized to require that the provider repay the patient, and could fine the provider. But this requires a truly independent ombudsman, and requires that patients are sufficiently well informed to be able to identify prima facie grounds for noncompliance with guidelines.

Detecting noncompliance is in any case hard with typical clinical guidelines, which are usually lengthy documents that are unintelligible to the average patient and full of discussion of variations of a "normal" case that a provider could point to in the event his clinical decisions are challenged. Clinical "pathways" are a promising way of cutting through this problem (AusAID Study Team 2007). Pathways are a simple document—a single form—that shows the steps to be taken treating a patient with a given diagnosis and how soon after admission the steps should be taken. At the end of each patient's bed lies a pathway form relevant to his or her condition. Whenever a doctor or other health worker provides care to the patient, it is recorded on the pathway form. The form is available for the patient to see, which improves his or her confidence that the provider will deliver care that is appropriate to the condition. But the pathways form can also be made available to the payer(s). When there is a single payer (for example, VSS in the universal coverage scenario), the pathways form provides a highly valuable tool for auditing. Bills can be linked to the diagnosis, and the care that has been delivered can be checked against the care package identified for a standard case in the pathway form. VSS would not need to audit every case. It would need to know the typical bill for a standard case for a given diagnosis (which it could obtain through statistical analysis of its billing database), and would look to the pathway only when the amount billed exceeded the "standard" bill by a given percentage. It could then determine whether the "off-pathway" care delivered appeared to be warranted. It might be that there were complications that warranted the extra care. But it might be that drugs and tests were administered that were not indicated and not required, or that tests were duplicated, or that care was not delivered at the appropriate time, and hence raised the cost of the case.

Pathways thus provide considerable scope for operationalizing clinical guidelines in a way that facilitates transparency in the relations between providers and patients, and providers and payers. They have been used in a number of countries, including other transition economies and Asian health systems. A study, for example, of the introduction of a clinical pathway for transurethral prostatectomy in a Taiwanese hospital found that after the introduction of the pathway, mean length of stay and admission charges both fell, in part due to a reduction in laboratory tests and drugs (Chang et al. 1998).

Clinical pathways are being developed specifically for Vietnam by MOH, with technical assistance by experts in the field and funding from the international donor community. To date, work on pathways has started for only a few diagnoses. The approach has been a bottom-up consultative process involving just a few large hospitals in Vietnam, and as yet there does not appear to be consensus on what the definitive Vietnamese clinical pathway for these conditions should look like. While this consultative approach has the merit of ensuring maximal buy-in from hospitals, it has the disadvantage of being slow. At this rate, it will be decades before Vietnamese pathways are available for the conditions that account for the bulk of hospital inpatient admissions. It might make sense, therefore, to begin with pathways developed in other countries, and have committees of experts (including representatives from senior hospital management) adapt them to the Vietnamese setting. It is also important that VSS be involved in the process, so that it can start to develop a pathway-based auditing system.

Provider Payment Reform

The need to reform the way that providers are paid has already been mentioned several times. The most obvious reforms are to shift to a case-based payment system (such as DRGs) for hospitals (with budget caps perhaps to limit volume), and a mix of capitation and FFS (for preventive interventions) for lower-level providers. As mentioned above, these changes could in principle be implemented in the current multiple-payer system where out-of-pocket payments dominate. However, as emphasized above, the reforms are far more likely to be successful in a single-payer system, that is, where VSS covers the entire population and pays for the bulk of health care costs.

Under a case-based payment system, the provider receives a predetermined amount of money, dependent on which diagnostic group the patient's diagnosis falls into. The number of groups varies from one country to the next: some have a few very broad (or "coarse") groups, while others have a large number of very narrow (or "fine") groups (Ellis and Miller 2008). Under case-based payment methods, hospitals have an incentive to treat extra cases, but also to contain their costs per case; the incentive is not to deliver more services *to existing patients*, as happens under FFS. On the plus side, too, DRGs may stimulate a shifting of care from a hospital setting to an outpatient clinic setting. This requires, however, that higher-level hospitals do not get DRG rates that are too generous. If the care provided is genuinely the same at different levels, rates should vary minimally between levels of hospitals. This may mean that higher-level hospitals would incur losses treating certain case types; this would be good, because it would encourage them to refer such cases downward to lower-level and lower-cost hospitals that can treat the patient just as well, but at a lower cost (AusAID Study Team 2007).

On the negative side, DRGs give providers an incentive to discharge patients early, to skimp on quality, and to select patients who are more profitable (the easier cases within each DRG, and the diagnoses with relatively profitable rates). DRGs can also lead to "gaming," as providers try to "upcode" cases, for example, claiming a standard delivery as a "delivery with complications" because it pays a higher rate. The incentive to select patients and game the system depends on the fineness of the DRG grouping: finer groupings (increasing the number of DRG groups) reduces the incentive to select patients, but increases the incentive to "upcode" patients (Ellis and Miller 2008). Some of these drawbacks can be tackled within the DRG system. There can be provisions, for example, for outliers (unusually expensive cases) to reduce skimping in costly cases. Clinical pathways are clearly a help here, too. The payer can monitor upcoding and apply stiff penalties. In addition, the payer may want to combine the case-based payment method with other payments. One approach being explored in the United States at the moment is to reward hospitals with additional payments if they score well on a battery of quality indicators (Nichols and O'Malley 2006). This system, known as pay-for-performance or P4P, is a supplementary payment method, not a replacement for case-based payments.

Case-based payment methods have been introduced in a large number of countries, including in East Asia (Wagstaff 2007c). In 2003, Japan introduced a payment system into 82 hospitals that is a mix of prospective payment and FFS (Okamura et al. 2005). The prospective component is case mix based, and is based on 2,552 groups that are part diagnosis-based and part procedure-based—hence the term "diagnosis-procedure combination" (DPC) groups. In 1997, Korea launched a pilot DRG program for inpatient care, covering nine disease categories (25 codes), which together accounted for 25 percent of inpatient cases (Kwon 2003). Korea's DRGs built in outlier payment features to reduce skimping. The scheme resulted in a 14 percent reduction in cost, a 6 percent reduction in average length of stay, and a substitution toward outpatient care away from inpatient care. No adverse effects on quality were found. In 2001, the pilot program was extended for the same disease categories to all hospitals. Taiwan has also taken steps to move away from FFS: A DRG system has been phased in for the 50 most common diseases.

Vietnam appears to be committed to case-based payments, and is exploring the feasibility of basing the rates on a cost analysis of the care associated with the clinical pathway for each case type (AusAID Study Team 2007). This approach has the merit over a statistical analysis of existing costs by case type of providing a "gold standard," indicating the costs associated with care delivered according to best practice clinical decision making. If some care at present is medically unnecessary, the "gold standard" will produce a payment per case type that is below the current average cost for that case type. The introduction of case-based payments would then result in hospitals incurring losses and would meet fierce resistance. Korea's strategy to get around this was to build in generous margins over the existing payment system (FFS) to overcome provider opposition (Kwon 2003). Over time, payment rates could gradually be reduced to their "gold standard" rates.

There is, however, a risk to building up a set of "gold standard" case-based payments based on Vietnam-specific clinical pathways, not least of which is that unless the model of developing Vietnamese pathways changes, pathways for the conditions that account for the bulk of inpatient admissions will not be ready for decades. One option would be to speed up the development of pathways along the lines suggested earlier, and stick with the idea of coming up with a gold standard case-based payment based on the resources required to deliver care according to the pathway. Another would be to take a DRG system that has been developed for another country (most have their origins in the United States' DRG system) (Schreyogg et al. 2006) and modify it to the Vietnamese setting. Over time, as the clinical pathways work proceeds in Vietnam and elsewhere, the DRG rates could be modified accordingly. One challenge here will be Vietnam's hospital information system. At present, it appears to be only a hospital-level database. Discharge-level records that include inter alia ICD-9-CM diagnosis and ICDOP procedure codes are not, it seems, available; hospitals are required to record this information, but the completed forms have never been computerized and their quality is unknown.

There is a need to develop an efficient and effective primary care system in Vietnam that will ensure that people are not admitted to the hospital with conditions that could have been treated in a nonhospital setting or prevented from occurring. This requires the development of a cadre of primary care physicians with offices staffed by appropriate support staff. They must be properly incentivized. Without appropriate incentives, primary care will not be a popular specialty among medical students, and the best doctors will continue to prefer to practice only in the cities. Capitation is likely to be one of the payment methods used, but people would need to be required to register with a first-level provider. In Vietnam currently, this is not required by VSS, though VSS could reduce its outlays by doing so, providing a network of primary care providers can be developed. The primary care provider would receive a fixed amount per patient for whom he is responsible, and would be liable for the costs of providing first-level care that his patients require. Estonia is a good example of the successful development of a primary care gatekeeper system (Koppel et al. 2003; Atun et al. 2006).

The capitation method could also be used for vertically integrated provider networks (for example, if a polyclinic were to join forces with the CHCs in its area and the village doctors to form an integrated service delivery network). The network as a whole in this case would receive the capitation payment. One approach, adopted by Thailand, is to pay hospitals a capitation fee. Given the costliness of hospital care, this gives the hospital an incentive to create a vertically integrated network of facilities below it that treats patients who can be treated at a lower-level facility instead of having patients self-refer to hospital.

Capitation gives primary care providers an incentive to attract more individuals who enroll with them. It also gives the primary care provider an incentive to reduce costs, because the lower the provider's costs per person on his list, the larger his net income. Primary care providers could reduce costs by, for example, employing nurse practitioners, and by doing some tests in-house rather than having them done by more expensive hospital labs. But a capitated first-level provider could also reduce costs by providing less care, or by selecting patients within each demographic grouping who are likely to require relatively little care (for example, young men) and discard others (for example, women of child-bearing age and the eld-erly). These potential risks can be reduced by weighting capitation rates according to the demographic characteristics of the provider's patient list, and by applying P4P to first-level providers. In the United Kingdom, an elaborate P4P scheme has been introduced to incentivize primary care physicians to deliver a variety of preventive measures (Doran et al. 2006).

Autonomy Reform

The quality and payment reforms suggested above are not contin-gent on there being a single payer, although they would be far more effective and easier to implement under a single-payer system. In contrast, the appropriate direction of reform in relation to provider autonomy does depend on the degree to which Vietnam is successful in its goal of universal coverage under a single payer.

With a single payer that picks up the bulk of health care costs, patients have a strong champion of their interests. If the payer has a quality control mechanism in place and a payment system that incen-tivizes cost containment and high quality (for instance, a mix of case-based payment and P4P), it makes good sense for health facilities to have a fairly strong financial incentive to treat more patients and improve quality. The payer would award contracts to facilities that meet the cost and quality standards of the payer, and the contracts would reward volume (extra cases, not extra services) and high qual-ity. In such a system, the scope for providers to earn additional income by delivering care that is medically unnecessary is limited. It is right and proper in such a system that providers should be incen-tivized to earn additional revenues, which they can do by treating extra patients and improving quality. Providers should also be encour-aged in this scenario to have a good deal of latitude over personnel and investment decisions. If they employ cheap but underqualified staff, they will risk forgoing quality-related payments. If they invest in expensive but unnecessary diagnostic equipment, they will incur additional costs that will not be covered by the case-based payment. With a strong "purchaser" and the right incentives, providers ought to be granted autonomy in most areas. It is no accident that countries shifting away from a budget-based payment system have also taken steps to autonomize health providers. In this scenario, Decrees 10 and 43 are very much along the right lines.

In contrast, in a system such as the present one in Vietnam, where the patient is the main payer, provider autonomy can spell disaster for the patient and the health system. Providers who are underqualified and deliver poor-quality care are less likely to be brought to account in such a system. Providers who invest in expensive equipment and deliver unnecessary diagnostic tests may fool patients into believing that they are providing high-quality care, while in reality they are merely increasing their incomes at the patients' expense.

China's health system during the 1990s and early 2000s provides a salutary reminder of what can happen when providers (even if nominally public) are given strong incentives to generate revenues in an environment where the patient is the main payer and oversight by the government is limited (Wagstaff and Lindelow 2008). It is not just that patients there pay a high fraction of the cost of care; the cost of care is high to start with, much higher relative to per-capita GDP than in other countries. It has been estimated that 20 percent of expenditures associated with the treatment of appendicitis and pneumonia are clinically unnecessary (Liu and Mills 1999). China has one of the highest shares of pharmaceutical expenditures in total health expenditure in the world—nearly 45 percent in 2003, compared to an average of around 15 percent in the OECD (Wagstaff and Lindelow 2008). One study of village clinics concluded that less than 1 percent of drug prescriptions were medically reasonable (Zhang et al. 2003). Caesarean sections have increased in China faster than can be explained by increases in risk factors (Cai et al. 1998). China has more MRI scanners per million people than Thailand and Mexico, which are considerably more affluent (Hutubessy et al. 2002).

Singapore's experience with hospital corporatization also serves as an important reminder of the limits of consumer-based competition in the health sector (Phua 2003; Wagstaff 2007c). The Singapore government created a single corporation, the Health Corporation of Singapore (HCS), under whose control around one-quarter of Singapore's hospitals were placed, accounting for nearly half of

Singapore's national bed stock. HCS, a holding company, is governed by private law, but is wholly owned by the government and answerable to the Ministry of Health. HCS can hire and fire staff and set terms of remuneration, and has considerable power to set prices. It is the residual claimant, though the government continues to cover any deficit through a subsidy, albeit on the understanding the subsidy will diminish over time. Cost recovery increased in Singapore's corporatized hospitals, achieved by raising prices; the government was forced, in the end, to impose limits on average charges per patient day. One newly corporatized hospital took the opportunity of reform to eliminate the class of beds intended for low-income patients whose occupants receive similar medical care but have only basic "hotel" facilities and pay only 80 percent of the cost. Physician earnings increased in the corporatized hospitals, and in order to stem the brain drain from unreformed hospitals to reformed hospitals, the government was forced to allow unreformed hospitals to set their own fees as well. The reforms precipitated considerable upward pressure on doctors' salaries throughout the system, but especially on those of surgeons. Concerns have also been voiced about a reform-induced scramble to acquire the latest technology, and the dumping of patients by corporatized hospitals on the uncorporatized sector.

The lesson for Vietnam is that the appropriate path for autonomization reforms hinges crucially on the degree to which Vietnam moves to a single payer that picks up the lion's share of health care costs. If this happens quickly, autonomization reforms along the lines of Decrees 10 and 43 make a good deal of sense. If not, the ongoing autonomization of government providers is likely to contribute to Vietnam's service delivery problems, not help to resolve them. Costs will continue to escalate, and high-quality care will continue to be elusive. Provider reforms cannot sensibly proceed independently of insurance reform.

CHAPTER 7

Decentralization and Government Stewardship

In any health system two key issues are: what should government do, and what roles should different ministries and different levels of government play? Vietnam is no exception. And like many other countries, Vietnam seems likely to end up reassessing many of the assignments of responsibilities in the years to come. As is apparent from the previous chapters, the health sector has been swept along on a number of economywide reforms over the years, including the introduction of a private sector, decentralization, and greater autonomy for public service delivery organizations. It has also promulgated some path-breaking reforms of its own, most notably the introduction of fees and drug sales in public facilities, and health insurance.

Yet the Ministry of Health and the health departments of provincial governments still see themselves essentially as the financier and operator of the supply side of the health system, despite the fact that much of the supply side is not public, that much of the public sector enjoys considerable autonomy, and that providers are increasingly drawing their revenues from insurance reimbursements and out-of-pocket spending rather than supply-side subsidies. Furthermore, the central government has been slow to respond to the decentralization of power to the province. The Health Ministry acts as if the health sector is simply administratively deconcentrated as before, and can be expected to follow central directives. To some degree, the behaviors of local government mirror this behavior of the central government. Local health officials still look to MOH as their guardian and "clan" leader, although by law they are answerable to local political and administrative officials. And the provinces do not always have the necessary appreciation, information, capacity, and motivation to discharge their health functions. They may expect the MOH to guide them, support them, or make up for their own failures. But in some areas, most notably in the implementation of Decision 139, provinces have demonstrated clearly that while they will look to MOH for guidance, they will not always act on it.

Current Health Responsibilities of Government in Vietnam

The government is currently heavily involved in the financing and delivery of health care. As far as finance is concerned, the government provides budget support to government facilities, collects mandatory contributions to the health insurance scheme, finances in full or in part the coverage of selected groups, and finances public health programs. Much of the financing comes from local governments, and local governments enjoy considerable autonomy in their spending decisions, including how much to spend across programs, and how much to allocate to the various units within the local government. But central government's role is not inconsequential. It provides transfers to the provinces that are used to support the various programs, including transfers for the Health Care Fund for the Poor program. Transfers from the central government to provinces are considerable: Some poorer provinces in the north receive grants that exceed 50 percent of their GDP (World Bank 2007). So, while provinces account for around 60 percent of all health spending (World Bank 2005), some of this (indeed much of it in the case of poorer provinces) is financed through transfers from Hanoi. Finally, part of the budgetary support that government provides to health facilities is central government budgetary support to its own facilities.

Responsibilities are somewhat fragmented at each level of government, too. The MOF manages the tax-transfer process that provides the resources that local governments use to provide budget support to public facilities and to pay the health insurance agency (VSS) for subsidized enrollees. VSS collects the mandatory (and voluntary) contributions to the health insurance program, then pools these with the subsidies from the MOF, and pays the providers for care received by people covered by VSS. However, MOLISA identifies beneficiaries for the Health Care Fund for the Poor. Finally, the ministry or department of health provides the budget support to its facilities out of its budget allocation from the ministry or department of finance. It would seem that the coordination of these various activities is not as good as it might be.

As far as the delivery of care is concerned, the government is the owner of a vast network of facilities. Again, local governments are most involved: central government operates less than 1 percent of health facilities, which contain only 7 percent of beds. Communes have the largest share of facilities (80 percent), but provinces have the largest share of beds (37 percent). The degree to which these facilities are directly managed by government has, of course, fallen with the passage of Decrees 10 and 43. However, they are still government-owned and -operated facilities, and the Ministry of Health and the departments of health continue to see the delivery of health care as one of their key responsibilities.

The government in Vietnam—as in other countries—also plays a role as steward of the health sector. But as in other countries, the government plays a more active role in some areas than others. It is active in developing policy, assuring the safety of medicines, regulating the fees that public providers can charge, and developing clinical guidelines for public facilities, among other things. It also licenses private providers, though not all private providers appear to be licensed. In reality, the government in Vietnam—like the governments of most other developing countries—in general has not played an active role in quality assurance or regulation of the private sector.

The central government also plays a stewardship function with respect to local governments, providing guidelines and technical assistance, particularly in respect to central transfers that are intended for specific national programs such as the Health Care Fund for the Poor program and the public health initiatives that fall under the national target programs. In principle, the ability of the central government to shape local government decision making in these areas ought to be considerable because it is ultimately the financier of these programs. In practice, its influence is rather weak. For example, as mentioned in chapter 1, central government requested that provinces enroll Decision 139 beneficiaries in the regular health insurance program rather than giving them a health card entitling them to subsidized care. Yet many provinces opted for the direct reimbursement modality.

The Future Horizontal Division of Responsibilities

The future division of responsibilities across government departments at each level of government seems likely to change over the next few years. The government has committed itself to reducing the system's reliance on out-of-pocket spending in favor of a subsidized public health insurance program that will ultimately cover everyone. It has committed itself to giving public providers greater freedom in a variety of decision-making spheres, and to further developing the private sector and allowing it to contract with the public insurance agency. At the same time, the government has signaled its commitment to raising the quality of care, including reducing the amount of unnecessary care being delivered, and remains firmly committed to public health.

These changes point toward an increased role for demand-side subsidies, with the government increasingly subsidizing public (and private) providers indirectly via the health insurance agency, and a reduced role for supply-side subsidies, with a gradual shift away from direct budget support of public facilities that provide clinical care. The role of the MOH and provincial health departments as a financier of health facilities would be much reduced. The emphasis on autonomization also implies a reduced role for the MOH and DOH as a direct manager of the network of providers delivering clinical care. These changes imply, however, an increased role for the MOH as overseer or steward of the system. This would entail oversight functions in relation to both the health insurance agency and the provider network. The strong commitment to public health also implies a continuation of the ministry's role as financier of public health programs, but also as the lead agency in the public health system.

The Health Ministry's role is thus likely to change considerably as Vietnam progresses on its reform path: it will become less and less a financier and manager of providers, and more and more a steward of the clinical services side of the health system, as well as continuing its traditional role of financier and operator of the public health system. The health insurance agency VSS, in contrast, will become less a passive payer of bills and more and more a purchaser of health care for its members, contracting with providers and paying them in a way that incentivizes high-quality care at a reasonable cost. This will require a sizable change of approach by VSS, and an upgrading of capacity and information systems. Providers will gradually acquire—through the implementation of Decrees 10 and 43—increased decision-making powers regarding the scale of their operation, merging vertically and horizontally with other providers, determining the size and composition of their staff, investing in new equipment, and so on.

What functions would a Health Ministry perform as steward of the system and as lead agency in the sphere of public health? The thinking on precisely what a government should be doing in public health has evolved over the last 20 years or so. There is an emphasis nowadays on clarifying public health functions, settling on the activities needed to perform these functions, and clarifying who should do what. Countries and international organizations have differed in how core public health functions have been defined, but common elements include prevention and control of disease and injuries, protection against environmental hazards and other health risks not related to disease, and public health disaster preparedness and response. Public health functions are sometimes defined more expansively to include, for example, quality control and assurance, equity, and human resources. While there may be a case for government intervention to address these issues, it is arguably a function of the health system as a whole, and not specifically a public health function.

Within the core areas, there is general agreement that the government should finance the activities, and deliver most of them through a dedicated public health system. This is certainly true of most population-based activities, such as surveillance. It is less true of personal public health interventions (such as immunization), which can be delivered by regular health providers, even if the interventions are publicly financed. The question then becomes whether it makes sense for the MOH (or its public health arm) to contract with providers itself, or whether it should pay the health insurer to include these interventions in its benefit package and simply monitor the insurer to make sure the interventions get delivered. With the evolving role of the Health Ministry, now might be a good time to undertake a review of public health functions in Vietnam, the activities undertaken in respect to them, and the spending involved, with a view to assessing coherence, efficiency, and adequacy.

As steward of the clinical services side of the health system, the MOH will remain the ultimate overseer of the system. It will not, however, be the only "actor" performing an oversight function in the health system. The insurer will play an oversight function regarding providers through its relations with them—it will continue its certification procedure for providers, rejecting those who fail to meet certain standards; it will begin to be more aggressive in setting down quality standards that contracted providers are expected to meet; it will want to check that care is being delivered according to the agreed standards; and so on. Health care professionals themselves are likely to play an oversight role in regard to their own activities. In many countries, they form themselves into associations, one function of which is to promote good clinical practice through dissemination of studies and results (many have their own journals), and through regulation of the membership (many have procedures for investigating and censuring members whose clinical activities deviate from agreed norms).

Provider organizations often have boards to which the management is answerable; the boards may reflect a diverse group of stakeholders and professionals, including members of the local community served by the facility, local government officials, and professionals in relevant fields such as medicine, accounting, and finance. The health insurance agency may also have its own board—this is the case in several semiautonomous social health insurance agencies around the world. Finally, entities outside the health system also have a role to play in the oversight of the system. In some countries, consumer groups act as "watchdogs," publishing surveys (increasingly via the Internet) of consumer experiences in the health system, whether at the hands of providers or at the hands of the health insurer. Where patients are given explicit rights and there are targets with respect to, say, acceptable delays for elective surgery, this can be an effective process. The MOH can play an important role in facilitating these various activities—setting down rules, for example, in relation to hospital and health insurer boards; assembling an explicit list of insurer and patient rights; and facilitating the development of professional medical associations.

While health professionals, boards, the public, and so forth are likely to play an important part in overseeing the health system, and while the Health Ministry can help promote their involvement there is still a need for the MOH to operate as the "grand" overseer of the system. Most fundamentally, it is the MOH—in concert with other ministries—that will be the custodian of health sector policy. It will not necessarily be the implementing agency for all aspects of policy, but it will be the lead ministry on making policy and thinking through its execution, including clarifying roles and responsibilities of different actors in the system. This will require that the ministry strengthen its research capacity, and its network with academic institutions and other knowledge providers within and outside the health sector, in order to have their inputs and other support in policy making, implementation, assessment, review, and reform. It will also entail the Health Ministry providing evidence to other central ministries about the health consequences of governmentwide reforms, and in the process influence health-related decrees and directives.

The Health Ministry will be responsible, too, for developing the "mortar" that binds the system together. The insurer might certify providers, but it is the MOH that will license them, and quite probably accredit them as well—in fact, the health insurer presumably ought to be required to certify and contract with only licensed providers. The Health Ministry will likely be the actor that develops clinical guidelines and pathways. It will likely be involved in the design of any prospective payment system, though probably not the only actor involved—the insurance agency is likely to be a key actor too. The MOH—in consultation with the insurer—will be the lead agency in developing a benefit package. And so on. These roles appear to be envisaged by Decree 63/2005.

In addition to designing and putting in place the tools the system uses on a day-to-basis (licensing, accreditation, clinical guidelines and pathways, and so on), the Health Ministry will have a key role to play in overseeing the activities of the various actors, and their interactions. It will enforce the licensing and accreditation system. It will make sure that insurers and providers are indeed employing the guidelines correctly and effectively, and that the insurer is covering the population it is supposed to cover, delivering services in the agreed benefit package, paying providers in a timely and fair way, and so on.

It will also have a role to play in overseeing the fee-paying private sector, which is likely to grow to include hospitals catering to the better-off, and in developing policies regarding private insurance. Many low-level private providers will not be contracted by the insurance agency, but will doubtless continue to provide care on a fee-paying basis. The MOH will have a responsibility to monitor and help improve the quality of care in this sector, which, as mentioned in chapter 1, appears to be lagging behind that in the public sector.

And finally, the Health Ministry will have a key role as the health sector's public information agency. It will need to ensure that people know of their entitlements in regard to insurance. As was seen in chapter 3, many currently do not. It will need to make people more aware that branded foreign drugs are no more effective on the whole than domestic generics, even though they are far more costly. Of course, many of the government's population-based public health activities entail the provision of information—advice to quit smoking, and so on.

More generally, the Health Ministry will have an important advocacy role—creating public awareness and interest, harnessing stakeholders' support, and providing strategic visions and directions. The MOH should extend its sphere of influence beyond government health workers to include more consumer groups and private sector representatives. The resolution of many of the problems now encountered, from underutilization of health services to the provision of counterfeit drugs to high prices of medical procedures, would involve private individuals, as patients or service providers.

The Future Vertical Division of Responsibilities

It is not just the horizontal allocation of roles that will change in the future—the allocation across different levels of government will likely change, too. Currently, the responsibilities are allocated in a somewhat ad hoc way, and the de jure allocation differs from the de facto allocation. Health insurance was recentralized in 2005, presumably with the intention of moving to a nationwide risk pool. Yet, as noted in chapter 1, because revenues per enrollee vary geographically less than expenditures, this creates perverse incentives as pointed out by the National Assembly's Committee for Social Affairs: A poor province lacking expensive high-tech equipment would likely run a surplus, which would end up covering the deficit of a rich province spending in excess of its revenues due to its costly high-tech care. Furthermore, the fact that risk is pooled nationally reduces the incentives for local governments to contain costs—they can simply pass on higher costs to the country as a whole. There are other examples. The health insurance scheme for the poor is supposed to be a nationwide program, and is financed largely by the central government. Yet many provinces have—against the express wishes of the central government—opted for the "direct reimbursement" modality rather than the insurance modality. Finally, national target programs (NTPs) are financed by the central government with the aim of ensuring a common approach and effort across the entire country on the challenges the programs address. Yet because the programs are financed through block grants over which provincial governments have some discretion in their use, not all local governments pursue the NTPs equally vigorously (World Bank 2005).

How will the move from supply-side to demand-side health financing play out with respect to the vertical allocation of responsibilities? Currently, local governments have revenue-raising authority, and the revenues are used to finance inter alia supply-side subsidies to the health sector. Intergovernmental transfers even out the differences in supply-side subsidies, but do not eliminate them. Contributions to the mandatory insurance scheme are higher in richer areas because earnings are higher, but contributions to the voluntary scheme vary much less. All revenues are pooled nationally, and returned to the province according to the outlays incurred. These outlays, as noted above, may well be higher in richer areas. This is partly because people in better-off areas are more likely to seek care, and to seek it from higher-level providers. But it also reflects the fact that providers are paid fee-for-service and those in richer areas have more high-tech equipment and can therefore deliver more tests and interventions per episode of treatment. In effect, richer areas have a more generous benefit package, even though the voluntarily insured pay a premium that is not much different from the premium paid by a voluntarily insured person in a poorer province.

If providers were paid on a prospective (fixed cost per case) basis, and providers were allowed to use any surpluses to upgrade their facilities, things would change. Insurance revenues would be less likely to get "transferred" from poor, low-cost areas to rich, high-cost ones, and rich areas—which would contribute more, at least in the contributory scheme—would see higher reimbursements only insofar as utilization rates were higher. This would significantly narrow inequalities in per capita health spending across different parts of Vietnam, and would leave richer provinces powerless to choose to spend part of their extra wealth on more generous health coverage. Such a step might be considered too radical a departure from the current practice of allowing richer provinces to spend more on health if they wish to do so, providing they contribute to the intergovernmental tax-sharing and transfer mechanism.

A way of "squaring the circle" would be to allow some differences in de facto benefit packages by reimbursing providers in richer areas on a higher fixed-cost basis. The quid pro quo would have to be commensurately higher contribution levels and rates in richer areas. In practical terms, the way forward might be a nationally mandated minimum level of spending per capita for the benefit package, with corresponding contribution requirements. The revenues would be pooled nationally, and reimbursements would be based on a common cost per case. In addition, provinces could be allowed—perhaps up to a maximum amount per capita—to operate a more generous benefit package than the minimum requirement, financed through commensurately higher contributions, and involving supplemental payments to providers over the basic rate. The supplemental contributions would not be pooled nationally but retained in a provincial fund, and would have to cover the extra costs incurred by the province opting for a more generous package than the national minimum. Local governments could thus have some decision-making power over revenue generation and health spending in a largely insurance-financed health system. The shift to an insurance system need not pose a threat to the principle of local preferences being accommodated, which underpins Vietnam's decentralization.

In other areas, however, the future logical role of local government would seem to be much more one of policy implementer rather than policy maker—a role that the World Bank's 1996 Public Expenditure Review advocated for basic health services (World Bank 1996). It would make sense for the central government to determine the basic benefit package amount; the financing of the package (including who will be subsidized, and ultimately whether the system should be financed through contributions or taxes); the rules governing provider autonomy, payments to providers, and the certification, licensing, and accreditation thereof, and so on. It would also make sense for central government to be developing a *national* public health strategy rather than having each province devise its own. In contrast, it would make sense for local governments to focus on implementing the rules of the game set by the center, with guidance and technical assistance from the center.

The fact that provinces would have the power to choose to raise revenues and spend above the basic package would provide them with a strong incentive to implement the rules of the system well, because part of the money being spent in the province will be seen as "its own," and inefficiencies in the system will reduce what the province achieves with "its" money. Would this be enough to encourage them to agree to a redrawing of the responsibilities between central and local government in the health area? Probably not. The central government would require other tools to persuade local governments to implement policy effectively.

One important set of tools available to the central government is the use of performance-based monitoring, evaluation, and awards. This would involve a shift to the use of output-based or outcome-based measures to monitor and evaluate the health performance of the local governments, and to use MOH resources and its access to donor resources to leverage improved local government performance. The leveraging framework could include contractual arrangements with local governments to perform desired tasks and achieve predetermined targets, in exchange for some "rewards" (technical assistance, budget support, honors, and recognition). This will also entail strengthening the accountability mechanisms in health through the education of consumers, civil service reforms, enhancing the oversight capacity of the People's Council and nongovernmental organizations, and better regulation. The MOH needs to become equally adept at monitoring compliance and devising ways to promote it as it is currently in issuing decrees.

Notes

1. Data from the IMF Statistical Appendix for Vietnam dated September 13, 2007.

2. International practice is to classify all out-of-pocket payments as private, whether they are to public or private providers. In Vietnam, by contrast, out-of-pocket payments to public providers are typically classified as public. International practice is also to classify SHI contributions as part of general government health expenditure (GGHE), and in this report this practice is followed. When the term "government health expenditure" is used, what is meant strictly is GGHE, including SHI contributions. Whether contributions by the voluntarily enrolled ought to be classified as part of GGHE is less clear. The program is government run, but the contributions are not mandatory, suggesting that they ought probably to be classified as private expenditures. In any event, in Vietnam, they are rather small, and whether they are classified as private health spending or as GGHE makes little difference.

3. See staff report for the IMF's Article IV consultation on Vietnam for 2007, and the IMF's Vietnam executive director's statement on the report.

4. The index values have actually been normalized by dividing the index by the relevant bound to take into account the fact that when the variable whose inequality is being investigated is bounded, the concentration index is also bounded. (Wagstaff 2005).

5. The reduction in inequality in Indonesia may have been caused at least in part by the crisis that hit the middle-income groups especially hard.

6. There are, of course, indirect costs as well, i.e., the lost earnings associated with ill health. (Wagstaff 2007a).

7. It is not clear whether this is due to a change in survey methodology between 2002 and 2004. The health spending modules were fairly similar. However, the 2002 survey gives far fewer outpatient visits per capita than the 2004 survey (20 percent of the 2004 figure), but far more inpatient visits (150 percent of the 2004 figure).

8. Services explicitly listed as covered are: (a) medical consultation, diagnosis and treatment, and rehabilitation (in the list of services approved by the MOH) while having treatment at health facilities; (b) laboratory tests, functional examination, imaging diagnosis; (c) drugs listed by the MOH; (d) blood and transfusion; (e) operations; (f) antenatal examination and delivery; (g) utilization of medical equipment and hospital beds. Services

explicitly not covered are: (a) treatment of leprosy; (b) specific drugs for the treatment of tuberculosis, malaria, schizophrenia, epilepsy, and other diseases if the costs have been covered by the state budget via national health programs, projects, or other financial sources; (c) the diagnosis and treatment of HIV/AIDS (except HIV tests prescribed by doctors and treatment of patients defined in Decision No. 265/2003/QD-TTg dated December 16, 2003, of the prime minister concerning policy for people exposed to HIV or infected by HIV/AIDS as a result of occupational risks), gonorrhea, and syphilis; (d) vaccination, convalescence, early detected pregnancy tests, medical checkup, including periodical checkup, examination of health to recruit laborers, for recruitment for the army and universities; family planning services and treatment of infertility; (e) prosthesis, aesthetic surgery; costs of artificial arm, leg, tooth, glasses, hearing aid; (f) treatment of occupational diseases; accidents at work (at the work place, during working hours or while working overtime required by employers or not at the work place while doing tasks assigned by employers; accidents that happen on the way to or back from work); injuries caused by the war or natural disasters; (g) treatment of cases of suicide, self-inflicted injuries; drug addiction, or injuries resulted from offenses against the law; h) Medical appraisal, forensic appraisal, mental examination; (i) medical treatment, rehabilitation, and diagnosis at the patients' residence; (j) drugs not included in the lists stipulated by the MOH, drugs consumed on special requirement of patients; utilization of treatment methods not yet permitted by the MOH; (k) participants in research and clinical experiments.

9. These figures are lower than the official VSS figures. It is not clear why.

10. Workers in international organizations and international NGOs are presumably covered by their employers' schemes.

11. In 2006, according to MOH's Health Statistics Yearbook, only 30 percent took place in a hospital or polyclinic.

12. See also Trivedi 2003 on this issue. He uses data from the 1997–98 Vietnam Living Standards Survey (VLSS).

13. In 2006, according to VSS data, just over 6 million were enrolled in the formal sector worker health insurance scheme, while about 6.5 million were in the compulsory pensions program. The latter includes, however, government officials, military personnel, and public security employees, some or all of whom may be classified as "meritorious persons" by VSS in their health insurance statistics.

14. Households in Colombia wanting to benefit from subsidized health insurance apply to have their means assessed, which involves a government official visiting the house and recording information on 15 indicators of living standards. These include the home appliances owned by the household, its

water source, the schooling of the head of the household, the household's social security status, and the demographic structure of the household. It even includes measures of household income and expenditure, though many countries settle for income proxies rather than income itself, resulting in a proxy means test. These 15 indicators are then aggregated in Colombia's case through Principal Components Analysis.

15. The assumptions are as follows. First, all 82.48 million Vietnamese would be covered. Second, once insured, people's utilization rates of outpatient and inpatient care would be 1.427 visits and 0.128 admissions per person. These are the rates among the insured in the 2006 VHLSS. Third, each outpatient visit and inpatient admission would cost, on average, D 44,000 and D 649,000, respectively (the VSS unit costs for 2006).

16. The impact on out-of-pocket payments has been calculated based on (a) the change in the numbers insured (bigger increases in the middle of the income distribution given the current distribution of coverage); and (b) the impact of insurance on out-of-pocket payments. The latter is estimated at 18 percent on average, with higher percentage impacts in the bottom half of the income distribution. The relatively modest impact reflects larger (but still relatively modest) reductions of 30 percent to 35 percent on outpatient and inpatient care costs being diluted by a much smaller (and statistically insignificant) impact on drugs and related expenditures (including travel costs), and a positive impact on expenditures on medical equipment (e.g., hearing aids, medicine cabinets, sputum-taking equipment). These figures are obtained from an analysis of the 2006 VHLSS data.

17. See WHO's report at http://www.who.int/tobacco/statistics/tobacco_atlas/ en/.

18. VHWs had five major responsibilities, as follows: (a) health education and communication; (b) community hygiene and preventive health; (c) maternal and child health care; (d) first aid and basic curative care; (e) public health programs.

19. This uses a decomposition used typically to assess how far wage differences between men and women are due to differences in endowments (e.g., differences in education) and differences in returns to endowments.(Oaxaca 1973; Neumark 1988). The former are "explained" differences, and the latter "unexplained" differences. Specifically, a separate wage regression equation is run for men and women, and the wage gap is decomposed into a part due to differences in mean values of the covariates (the explained part), and a part due to differences in the coefficients (the unexplained part). The same approach is adopted here on a data set of Vietnam's hospitals. The regression is a cost function along the lines used first by Granneman et al. 1986, and subsequently by Weaver and Deolalikar 2004 in their study of hospital costs in Vietnam.

20. The following information was used to design this proposal: Studies on costs of delivering health care in 1991, 1992, and 1993, using data routinely collected by the Department of Planning and Finance and Department of Health Management of the MOH; a study on actual costs of 10 services in 10 hospitals, 1991-92; a survey on actual costs of treatment in Dong Anh Hospital, Hanoi, 1992, and of treatment in Viet-Tiep Hospital, Haiphong, 1993; an analysis of annual hospital budgets based on the inventory of hospitals collected by MOH's Department of Finance and Department of Treatment; actual hospital and clinic price levels; and experience from other countries in the region, such as Australia, Singapore, and Thailand.

21. The model is similar to that discussed by Wooldridge (Wooldridge 2002) on p. 317, except that there is no random time trend in our model. We estimate a fixed-effect model with a period-specific intercept and dummies capturing whether and how long a hospital has been autonomized. The model is estimated from data on the Decree 10/43 status of individual hospitals provided by MOH, and from hospital inventory data. Dependent variables are logs of total revenues, revenues from user fees, health insurance, budget, and other, all expressed on a per-case basis. The model also includes hospital-specific fixed effects, and is estimated on data for the years 2004 and 2005.

References

Ahmad, E. 2008. "Taxation Reforms and Sequencing of Intergovernmental Reforms in China: Preconditions for a Xiaokang Society." In *Public Finance in China: Reform and Growth for a Harmonious Society*, ed. Jiwei Lou and Shuilin Wang, 95–126. Washington, DC: World Bank.

Atun, R.A., N. Menabde, K. Saluvere, M. Jesse, and J. Habicht. 2006. "Introducing a Complex Health Innovation—Primary Health Care Reforms in Estonia (Multimethods Evaluation)." *Health Policy* 79 (1): 79–91.

AusAID Study Team. 2007. "Hospital Sector Study: Summary Report." Ministry of Health, Hanoi, Vietnam and Joint Health Policy Initiative .

Buntin, M.B., and A.M. Zaslavsky. 2004. "Too Much Ado about Two-Part Models and Transformation? Comparing Methods of Modeling Medicare Expenditures." *Journal of Health Economics* 23 (3): 525–42.

Cai, W., Y. Zhuang, J.S. Marks, C.H.C. Chen, L. Morris, and J.R. Harris. 1998. "Increased Caesarean Section Rates and Emerging Patterns of Health Insurance in Shanghai, China." *American Journal of Public Health* 88 (5): 777–80.

Chang, P.L., S.T. Huang, T.M. Wang, M.L. Hsieh, and K. H. Tsui. 1998. "Improvements in the Efficiency of Care after Implementing a Clinical-Care Pathway for Transurethral Prostatectomy." *British Journal of Urology* 81 (3): 394–7.

De Ferranti, D.M. 1985. "Paying for Health Services in Developing Countries: An Overview." World Bank staff working paper No. 721, Report No. 0821305026, World Bank, Washington, DC.

Docteur, E., and H. Oxley. 2003. *Health-Care Systems: Lessons from the Reform Experience*. Paris: Organisation for Economic Co-operation and Development.

Doran, T., C. Fullwood, H. Gravelle, D. Reeves, E. Kontopantelis, U. Hiroeh, and M. Roland. 2006. "Pay-for-Performance Programs in Family Practices in the United Kingdom." *New England Journal of Medicine* 355 (4): 375.

Ellis, R., and M. Miller. 2008. "Provider Payment Methods and Incentives." In *Encyclopedia of Public Health*, ed. K. Heggenhougen, 395–402. Oxford: Academic Press.

Escobar, M.L. 2005. "Health Sector Reform in Colombia." *Development Outreach* May: 6–9.

Fritzen, S.A. 2007. "Legacies of Primary Health Care in an Age of Health Sector Reform: Vietnam's Commune Clinics in Transition." *Social Science & Medicine* 64 (8): 1611–23.

Gertler, P., and O. Solon. 2000. *"Who Benefits From Social Health Insurance in Developing Countries?" Mimeo,* University of California at Berkeley, Berkeley, CA.

Glewwe, P. 2003. "An Overview of Economic Growth and Household Welfare in Vietnam in the 1990s." In *Economic Growth, Poverty and Household Welfare: Policy Lessons from Vietnam,* ed. P. Glewwe, N. Agrawal, and D. Dollar, 1–26. Washington, DC: World Bank.

Government of Vietnam-Donor Working Group on Public Expenditure Review. 2000. *Vietnam—Managing Public Resources Better. Public Expenditure Review.* Hanoi, Vietnam: Joint Review of the Government of Vietnam-Donor Working Group on Public Expenditure Review.

Grannemann, T.W., R.S. Brown, and M.V. Pauly. 1986. "Estimating Hospital Costs. A Multiple-Output Analysis." *Journal Health Economics* 5 (2): 107–27.

Gwatkin, D., S. Rutstein, K. Johnson, E. Suliman, and A. Wagstaff. 2003. *Socio-Economic Differences in Health, Nutrition and Population.* Washington, DC: World Bank.

Hussain, A., and N. Stern. 2008. "Public Finances, the Role of the State, and Economic Transformation, 1978–2020." In *Public Finance in China: Reform and Growth for a Harmonious Society,* ed. J. Lou and S. Wang, 13–38. Washington, DC: World Bank.

Hutubessy, R.C., P. Hanvoravongchai, and T.T. Edejer. 2002. "Diffusion and Utilization of Magnetic Resonance Imaging in Asia." *International Journal of Technology Assessment Health Care* 18 (3): 690–704.

Jowett, M., P. Contoyannis, and N.D. Vinh. 2003. "The Impact of Public Voluntary Health Insurance on Private Health Expenditures in Vietnam." *Social Science and Medicine* 56 (2): 333–42.

Jowett, M., A. Deolalikar, and P. Martinsson. 2004. "Health Insurance and Treatment Seeking Behaviour: Evidence from a Low-Income Country." *Health Economics* 13 (9): 845–57.

Knowles, J., T. Nguyen, B. Dang, K. Nguyen, T. Tran, K. Nguyen, and N. Vu. 2005. *Making Health Care More Affordable for the Poor: Health Financing in Vietnam.* Hanoi, Vietnam: Medical Publishing House.

Koppel, A., K. Meiesaar, H. Valtonen, A. Metsa, and M. Lember. 2003. "Evaluation of Primary Health Care Reform in Estonia." *Social Science and Medicine* 56 (12): 2461–6.

Kwon, S. 2003. "Payment System Reform for Health Care Providers in Korea." *Health Policy Planning* 18 (1): 84–92.

Lieberman, S.S., J.J. Capuno, and H.V. Minh. 2005. Decentralizing Health: Lessons from Indonesia, the Philippines, and Vietnam. *East Asia Decentralizes: Making Local Government Work.* World Bank. Washington, DC, World Bank: ix, 267.

Liu, X. and A. Mills. 1999. "Evaluating Payment Mechanisms: How Can We Measure Unnecessary Care?" *Health Policy and Planning* 14 (4): 409–13.

Mullahy, J. 1997. "Instrumental-Variable Estimation of Count Data Models: Applications to Models of Cigarette Smoking Behavior." *Review of Economics and Statistics* 79 (4): 586–93.

Neumark, D. 1988. "Employers' Discriminatory Behavior and the Estimation of Wage Discrimination." *Journal of Human Resources* 23 (3): 279–95.

Nichols, L.M., and A. S. O'Malley. 2006. "Hospital Payment Systems: Will Payers Like the Future Better than the Past?" *Health Affairs (Millwood)* 25 (1): 81–93.

Nyman, J.A. 1999. "The Economics of Moral Hazard Revisited." *J Health Econ* 18 (6): 811–24.

O'Donnell, O., E. van Doorslaer, R.P. Rannan-Eliya, A. Somanathan, S.R. Adhikari, D. Harbianto, C.G. Garg, P. Hanvoravongchai, M.N. Huq, A. Karan, G.M. Leung, C.-W. Ng, B.R. Pande, K. Tin, L. Trisnantoro, C. Vasavid, Y. Zhang, and Y. Zhao. 2007. "The Incidence of Public Spending on Healthcare: Comparative Evidence from Asia." *World Bank Economic Review* 21 (1): 93–123.

O'Donnell, O., E. van Doorslaer, R.P. Rannan-Eliya, A. Somanathan, C.G. Garg, P. Hanvoravongchai, M.N. Huq, A. Karan, G.M. Leung, K. Tin, and C. Vasavid. 2005. "Explaining the Incidence of Catastrophic Expenditures on Health Care: Comparative Evidence from Asia." EQUITAP Working Paper #5, Eramsus University, Rotterdam, the Netherlands, and IPS, Colombo, Sri Lanka.

Oaxaca, R. 1973. "Male-Female Wage Differentials in Urban Labor Markets." *International Economic Review* 14: 693–709.

Okamura, S., R. Kobayashi, and T. Sakamaki. 2005. "Case-Mix Payment in Japanese Medical Care." *Health Policy* 74 (3): 282–6.

Pannarunothai, S., D. Patmasiriwat, and S. Srithamrongsawat. 2004. "Universal Health Coverage in Thailand: Ideas for Reform and Policy Struggling." *Health Policy* 68 (1): 17–30.

Phua, K.H. 2003. "Attacking Hospital Performance on Two Fronts: Network Corporatization and Financing Reforms in Singapore." In *Innovations in Health Service Delivery: The Corporatization of Public Hospitals*, ed. A.S. Preker and A. Harding, 451–483. Washington, DC: World Bank.

Pritchett, L., and L.H. Summers. 1996. "Wealthier is Healthier." *Journal of Human Resources* 31 (4): 841–68.

Ramanan Laxminarayan, A. D. 2004. "Tobacco Initiation, Cessation, and Change: Evidence from Vietnam." *Health Economics* 13 (12): 1191–1201.

Schreyogg, J., T. Stargardt, O. Tiemann, and R. Busse. 2006. "Methods to Determine Reimbursement Rates for Diagnosis Related Groups (DRG): A

Comparison of Nine European Countries." *Health Care Management Science* 9 (3): 215–23.

Sepehri, A., R. Chernomas, and A.H. Akram-Lodhi. 2003. "If They Get Sick, They Are in Trouble: Health Care Restructuring, User Charges, and Equity in Vietnam." *International Journal of Health Services* 33 (1): 137–61.

Sepehri, A., S. Sarma, and W. Simpson. 2006a. "Does Non-profit Health Insurance Reduce Financial Burden? Evidence from the Vietnam Living Standards Survey Panel." *Health Economics* 15 (6): 603–16.

Sepehri, A., W. Simpson, and S. Sarma. 2006b. "The Influence of Health Insurance on Hospital Admission and Length of Stay—The Case of Vietnam." *Social Science and Medicine* 63 (7): 1757–70.

The Reforming States Group. 1998. "Balanced Federalism and Health System Reform. The Reforming States Group." *Health Affairs (Millwood)*, 17 (3): 181–91.

Thuan, N.T., C. Lofgren, N.T. Chuc, U. Janlert, and L. Lindholm. 2006. "Household Out-of-Pocket Payments for Illness: Evidence from Vietnam." *BMC Public Health* 6: 283.

Towse, A., A. Mills, and V. Tangcharoensathien. 2004. "Learning from Thailand's Health Reforms." *BMJ* 328 (7431): 103–05.

Trivedi, P. 2003. "Patterns of Health Care Use in Vietnam: Analysis of 1998 Vietnam Living Standards Survey Data." In *Economic Growth, Poverty and Household Welfare: Policy Lessons from Vietnam*, ed. P. Glewwe, N. Agrawal, and D. Dollar, 391–423. Washington, DC: World Bank.

Tuan, T., V.T.M. Dung, I. Neu, and M.J. Dibley. 2005. "Comparative Quality of Private and Public Health Services in Rural Vietnam." *Health Policy and Planning* 20 (5): 319–27.

Van Doorslaer, E., O. O'Donnell, R.P. Rannan-Eliya, A. Somanathan, S.R. Adhikari, B. Akkazieva, D. Harbianto, C.G. Garg, P. Hanvoravongchai, A.N. Herrin, M.N. Huq, S. Ibragimova, A. Karan, T.-j. Lee, G.M. Leung, J.-F. R. Lu, C.-w. Ng, B.R. Pande, R. Racelis, S. Tao, K. Tin, L. Trisnantoro, C. Vasavid, B.-m. Yang, and Y. Zhao. 2005. "Paying Out-of-Pocket for Health Care in Asia: Catastrophic and Poverty Impact." EQUITAP Working Paper #2, Erasmus University, Rotterdam, the Netherlands, and IPS, Colombo, Sri Lanka.

van Doorslaer, E., O. O'Donnell, R.P. Rannan-Eliya, A. Somanathan, S.R. Adhikari, C.C. Garg, D. Harbianto, A.N. Herrin, M.N. Huq, S. Ibragimova, A. Karan, T.J. Lee, G.M. Leung, J.F. Lu, C.W. Ng, B.R. Pande, R. Racelis, S. Tao, K. Tin, K. Tisayaticom, L. Trisnantoro, C. Vasavid, and Y. Zhao. 2007. "Catastrophic Payments for Health Care in Asia." *Health Economics* 16 (11): 1159–84.

Van Doorslaer, E., O. O'Donnell, R.P. Rannan-Eliya, A. Somanathan, S.R. Adhikari, C.C. Garg, D. Harbianto, A.N. Herrin, M.N. Huq, S. Ibragimova, A. Karan,

C.W. Ng, B.R. Pande, R. Racelis, S. Tao, K. Tin, K. Tisayaticom, L. Trisnantoro, C. Vasavid, and Y. Zhao. 2006. "Effect of Payments for Health Care on Poverty Estimates in 11 Countries in Asia: An Analysis of Household Survey Data." *Lancet* 368 (9544): 1357–64.

Van Kinh, H., H. Ross, D. Levy, N.T. Minh, and V.T.B. Ngoc. 2006. "The Effect of Imposing a Higher, Uniform Tobacco Tax in Vietnam." *Health Research Policy and Systems* 4 (1): 6.

Vietnam Ministry of Health/Health Partnership Group. 2008) *Joint Annual Health Review 2007*. Hanoi, Vietnam: Ministry of Health.

Wagstaff, A. 2005. "The Bounds of the Concentration Index When the Variable of Interest is Binary, with an Application to Immunization Inequality." *Health Economics* 14 (4): 429–32.

Wagstaff, A. 2007a. "The Economic Consequences of Health Shocks: Evidence from Vietnam." *Journal of Health Economics* 26 (1): 82–100.

Wagstaff, A. 2007b. "Health Insurance for the Poor: Initial Impacts of Vietnam's Health Care Fund for the Poor." Impact Evaluation Series #11. Policy Research Working Paper #WPS 4134, World Bank, Washington, DC.

Wagstaff, A. 2007c. "Health Systems in East Asia: What Can Developing Countries Learn from Japan and the Asian Tigers?" *Health Economics* 16 (5): 441–56.

Wagstaff, A., and M. Lindelow. 2008. "Health Reform in Rural China: Challenges and Options." In *Public Finance in China: Reform and Growth for a Harmonious Society*, eds. Jiwei Lou and Shuilin Wang, 265–286. Washington, DC: World Bank.

Wagstaff, A., and N.N. Nguyen. 2003. "Poverty and Survival Prospects of Vietnamese Children under Doi Moi." In *Economic Growth, Poverty and Household Welfare: Policy Lessons from Vietnam*. ed. P. Glewwe, N. Agrawal, and D. Dollar, 313–350. Washington, DC: World Bank.

Wagstaff, A., and M. Pradhan. 2005. "Health Insurance Impacts on Health and Non-Medical Consumption in a Developing Country." Policy Research Working Paper #3563, World Bank, Washington, DC.

Wagstaff, A., and E. van Doorslaer. 2003. "Catastrophe and Impoverishment in Paying for Health Care: With Applications to Vietnam 1993–1998." *Health Economics* 12 (11): 921–34.

Weaver, M., and A. Deolalikar. 2004. "Economies of Scale and Scope in Vietnamese Hospitals." *Social Science and Medicine* 59 (1): 199–208.

Witter, S. 1996. "Doi Moi' and Health: The Effect of Economic Reforms on the Health System in Vietnam." *International Journal of Health Planning and Management* 11 (2): 159–72.

Wooldridge, J.M. 2002. *Econometric Analysis of Cross Section and Panel Data*. Cambridge, MA: MIT Press.

World Bank. 1992. "Viet Nam—Population, Health and Nutrition Sector Review." Report #10289, World Bank, Washington, DC.

World Bank. 1996. "Viet Nam—Fiscal Decentralization and the Delivery of Rural Services: An Economic Report." Report No. 1 5745-VN, World Bank, Washington, DC.

World Bank. 2001. "Vietnam. Growing Healthy: A Review of Vietnam's Health Sector." Report No. 2221 0-VN, World Bank, Washington, DC.

World Bank. 2005. "Vietnam—Managing Public Expenditure for Poverty Reduction and Growth: Public Expenditure Review and Integrated Fiduciary Assessment." Report No. 30035, World Bank, Washington, DC.

World Bank. 2007. *Vietnam Development Report 2008: Social Protection*. Hanoi, Vietnam: World Bank.

World Health Organization. 1998. *Child Health and Development 1996–97 Report*. Geneva, Switzerland: World Health Organization.

Zhang, X., Z. Feng, and L. Zhang. 2003. "Analysis on Quality of Prescription of Township Hospitals in Poor Areas." *Journal of Rural Health Service Management* 23 (12): 33–35.

Index